CW00552856

MEDICINAL
SEASONINGS

Dr Keith Scott

MEDSPICE PRESS

Published by Medspice CC

PO Box 486
Simon's Town
Cape Town
7995
South Africa
www.medspice.com

Medicinal Seasonings

ISBN 0-620-35984-6

Cover design and photographs by John Peacock

Printed and bound by Formsxpress CC
5 Lily Road, Retreat, 7945, Cape Town

MEDICINAL
SEASONINGS

Contents

Foreword

The power pendulum of popular medicine is swinging back in the direction of natural, holistic approaches and *Medicinal Seasonings* is a testament to both the scientific and mental aspects of that shift. The wisdom of natural healing has, unfortunately, been omitted from the curricula of most medical schools where students are taught to focus on the treatment of symptoms using potentially dangerous drugs. In North America alone, adverse drug reactions are responsible for thousands of deaths every year whereas there has not been a single death attributed to culinary herbs and spices!

Medicinal Seasonings not only gives us insight into the wonderful healing powers of spices and the scientific proof of their mechanisms of action, it also arms us with a wealth of knowledge and proof that substantial elements of natural medicine have a scientific foundation. This book is based on firm scientific inquiry and represents countless hours of research. It should be read both for pleasure and for its useful content. It is clearly presented and makes fascinating reading, especially if one is looking for data on the important illnesses afflicting modern society. If you commit yourself to the use of more herbs and spices you will be rewarded with improved health and increased vitality and vigour. Delve in and explore what is offered here with enthusiasm and positivity. In this way you will not only improve your health but will help to prevent the onset of serious chronic diseases.

Lastly, Dr. Scott needs to be congratulated on his work which culminated in this book. He is not only well read and enthusiastic but the fact that he decided to share his knowledge makes it even more special. It was indeed a pleasure to read *Medicinal Seasonings* and an honour to write this foreword.

Patrick JD Bouic
Professor of Immunology
Stellenbosch University Medical School
South Africa

1

Preface

▶ **Health Alternatives**

When I graduated from medical school, I thought that I had access to an impressive arsenal of treatments that would enable me to heal most of the patients who walked through my office door. However, more and more time spent at the coal face began to make me realise that the orthodox medical tools given me, although highly effective when used to cure certain diseases, were limited in the extent to which they could treat many others. Complementary therapies and paying more attention to nutrition became important adjuncts in my medical practice, and these modalities helped many patients for whom orthodox treatment had been ineffective. However, serious conditions like cardiovascular disease, cancer, diabetes and others, once they had become established, were still difficult to manage without the use of expensive, often dangerous, drugs and surgery. The obvious strategy was to try to find ways to prevent these from occurring in the first place.

▶ **Limits to Preventive Medicine**

One of the foundations of modern health care is preventive medicine, but doctors pay much less attention to it than we care to admit; and trying to get even a proportion of our clients to adopt better living habits is an ongoing battle that many health workers find difficult to sustain. Good nutrition is one of the pillars of preventive medicine and is an aspect of health care in which I have always had an interest. Dietary manipulation for individuals with arthritis, heart disease, diabetes and cancer works to a certain degree depending, to some extent, on how rigorously patients stick to their diets. In addition, vitamin, mineral and other supplements such as essential fatty acids have had a positive impact on the health of some of these patients. However, I began to realise that in spite of all the

3

different treatment modalities available, some vital facet in the whole concept of preventive health care appeared to be missing. Treatment failures could conveniently be put down to the 'bad genes' of a particular patient but, genetic weaknesses notwithstanding, I was convinced that there was another dimension to health that was being overlooked.

▶ Lessons from the Kalahari Desert

It was not until I became aware of the habits and lifestyle of the San Bushmen, a nomadic, hunter-gatherer people whose remnants live in southern Africa's Kalahari Desert, that I began to get a glimpse of what now appears to be this elusive factor. For more than a decade I had a medical practice on the outskirts of this vast desert and had the good fortune to count some of these nomads as my patients. The lifestyle of these hardy desert dwellers, especially in relation to their health, was intriguing, and I began to take a closer look at their dietary habits. Several researchers had lived with and studied the Bushmen and had published a handful of books and academic papers on their research findings. One particular anthropologist, who had spent many years studying all aspects of their lives, had painstakingly documented all the foods that comprised the diverse diet of the San.

His research revealed that they ate a far greater variety of plant species than that provided by a typical Western diet. As a hunter-gatherer people the San roamed over large areas carrying very little food with them, relying instead on hunting animals and collecting various nuts, berries, roots, tubers, melons and other plants as they moved across the desert. This nomadic existence exposed them to a substantial variety of edible plant species that varied from season to season and from one micro-climate to another.

❯ Healthy, Strong-tasting Foods

Some of the plants found in the Kalahari are very tasty, but others are
bitter or sour and are usually only eaten when there is nothing more
palatable available. The concentration of different chemicals in the plants
also varies according to the seasons. In times of drought high levels of
compounds like phytoestrogens or strong-tasting flavonoids may be
found in a particular plant, but when the rains fall smaller quantities of
these compounds are produced by the same species. Even though many
of these plants are fairly unpalatable, for many months of the year the
Bushmen elect to either eat these less desirable foods or starve. If given
the choice they will, like all of us, prefer to eat the tastier foods rather than
the less palatable ones; but being forced to eat the often bitter, stronger-
flavoured plants they have, unknowingly, been ingesting foods that have
made a significant contribution to their excellent health. We now know
that it is often the harsher, sharper-tasting plants or parts of the plants
(like the skins) that contain biologically active phytochemicals; it is these
compounds that provide a wide range of vital health benefits.

❯ San Health and Longevity

Another remarkable feature of their lives is that, in their natural, nomadic
state, the average life expectancy of the San Bushman is about 65 years.
Considering the harsh environment in which they live and, up until
recently, their limited access to medical facilities, this degree of longevity
is unexpectedly high. My own experience of treating San patients
bore out these facts. Mostly I treated them for a variety of infections
that they acquired when they spent time in the villages or towns on
the periphery of the Kalahari. The information that I gleaned from
academic publications and the direct contact that I had with them was
confirmation that I needed to look further into what, to my mind, was a
"missing link" in preventive medicine.

▶ Plant Contraceptives

Although I realised that the variety of food species that the Bushmen ate must have something to do with their healthy longevity, I first assumed that it was because these foods provided them with a full range of essential nutrients. In addition, by the very nature of their lifestyle, they had plenty of exercise and obesity was unknown amongst them. An interesting piece of research then caught my eye. An ethno-botanist had analysed the chemical constituents of several berries at different times of the year and had found that in times of drought those berries produced far greater amounts of plant oestrogens than they did when there was normal rainfall. Another researcher had noted that San women had few pregnancies during times of drought. They tended to conceive more frequently during the rainy summer and autumn months than during the more famine-prone seasons of winter and spring. Putting these two facts together led me to question whether the phytoestrogens were in fact having a similar effect on the body as the oestrogen-based oral contraceptive pill. Scientists have since found that high levels of plant oestrogens can indeed reduce the fertility of certain animal species, but this effect has yet to be shown in humans.

▶ A Missing Link?

The possibility that plant-based chemicals could influence human health to the extent that they may prevent a woman from falling pregnant at a time of food shortage suggested that there may be other noteworthy properties provided by a varied diet such as this. I began to search for further evidence that might support my suspicion that there were other phytochemicals that could influence human physiology; compounds that might provide protection against specific diseases or other environmentally induced stresses. After all, the Bushmen lived a full lifespan in a harsh environment while suffering few of the degenerative diseases we see in the West today, and this could not be entirely attributed to a "stress-free" lifestyle.

The closer I looked into this field of research the more I began to realise that what we generally consider a normal, balanced diet does not in itself provide everything we need to lead healthy lives. If we have all the nutrients we need for growth, energy storage and repair, we will indeed be healthy up to a point. However, even if we fastidiously eat what is generally accepted as a "balanced diet" and take nutritional supplements, we will probably still be lacking in certain important dietary factors. "Balanced", perhaps; adequate, unlikely. The reason is that we require more than just the basic nutrients to stay healthy. We need the medicinal substances that can be found in certain plant species; and we should eat them all of the time - not only when we become ill. These vital compounds can be found in a variety of plants that humans and animals have been eating for millennia, and the secret is that the most important of these are found in the culinary spices that some societies have incorporated into their recipes for thousands of years.

❱ Scientific Confirmation

Scientists are discovering increasing numbers of plant-based substances that *do* protect us against many diseases ranging from infections to heart disease, Alzheimer's disease, diabetes and cancer. In many countries, especially the developed nations, we have gradually reduced the variety and quantity of plant species that we include as dietary staples. It is my contention (and there is an increasing body of scientific evidence to support this view) that if we re-introduce enough of these spicy, flavour-some plants into our diets, we will add a whole new dimension to the practice of preventive medicine. There is more and more evidence that the piquant flavours and rich colours found in some plants are the clues that lead us to a huge treasure-trove of life-enhancing, disease-preventing phytochemicals. As researchers continue to unearth more and more of these important plant substances and identify the ways in which they help to keep us fit and healthy, so epidemiologists are showing us that certain population groups have lower incidences of heart disease, cancer, Alzheimer's disease, diabetes and other illnesses. The low prevalence of these disorders is a result of the regular consumption of the parent spices, herbs, vegetables and fruits that hold these vital compounds. A key element of these spice-consuming societies' good health is that, in most cases unknowingly, they are self-medicating on a daily basis. At every meal they swallow large quantities of chemicals that protect them against many diseases. They enjoy taking these "drugs" not because they are hypochondriacs but because these substances are an integral part of the cuisine that they have been weaned on. They continue to use strongly flavoured plant foods similar to those that our hunter-gatherer ancestors ate as they wandered from one hunting ground to another. Now they cultivate these plants and incorporate them into their recipes, but the health benefits are the same. These remarkable foods continue to provide a potent, protective umbrella of health to those who use them regularly and in sufficient quantities.

In this book I attempt to draw together the results of epidemiological, laboratory and clinical studies that provide overwhelming evidence to show why certain food types, especially the spices, are valuable sources of the hundreds of phytochemicals that should play a major role in helping to prevent the onset of some of our most troublesome, costly and lethal degenerative diseases.

Acknowledgements

If it had not been for the work of anthropologists, epidemiologists, biochemists, botanists, ethno-botanists, doctors and other researchers I would have been unable to produce this book. Scientists such as these continue to unearth the hard evidence that shows how and why plant compounds play such a valuable role in protecting us against so many degenerative and other diseases. Long may they continue to provide us with the incontrovertible facts we need to confirm how important spices and other plant compounds are to our health.

I would also like to thank Linda McCourt for her expert advice on matters nutritional and for helping me to do the research for this book. Thanks to Peter and Sandi Unite for providing support over the many months that it took to produce this volume.

I would also like to acknowledge the invaluable contributions made by my editor, Christine Didcott, and Katya Soggot, who proof read the manuscript. My appreciation too for the wonderful job Abdul Amien did in typesetting and designing the interior of the book.

Thanks to John Peacock for all the work he put in to produce such stunning photographs and cover designs.

Extra special thanks, however, go to my daughter, Robyn Scott who devoted an enormous amount of her valuable time improving both the readability of the manuscript and for providing me with invaluable criticism of its content. Without her scientific knowledge, journalistic talent and selfless dedication, I would not have been able to produce a book of this quality.

PART 1

THE BIG PICTURE

Introduction

CHAPTER 1

The Purpose of *Medicinal Seasonings*

Much has been written on the uses of herbs and spices in traditional and folk medicine, therefore their uses in this regard are not included in this book. All the foods that appear here are commonly used culinary spices, and those herbs that are used exclusively for medicinal purposes have been excluded from the book. The intention is to provide useful information to those who are looking for ways to protect themselves against the degenerative diseases that are the scourge of most developed countries and their aging populations. Although some spices do have a strong history of use as traditional medicines, it is the scientific research into their preventive and curative properties that is the focus of the following chapters. This approach should in no way suggest that the traditional uses are invalid, only that they have yet to be confirmed by modern research.

The wide array of antioxidants and other phytochemicals found in spices have potent protective effects against cancer, heart disease, diabetes, obesity, Alzheimer's disease and can slow the aging process too. In order to focus on the preventive aspect of health, as much of the available scientific evidence is presented to show how and why spices are so important in our fight against these prevalent disorders. In this respect *Medicinal Seasonings* is more a "how to prevent" volume rather than a "how to treat" book.

Definition of a Spice

The word spice has several definitions, but for the purpose of this book a spice is defined as:

"an aromatic substance used as a food flavouring"

This definition includes foods like chilies, ginger, garlic, pepper, etc. that we traditionally refer to as "spices", as well as oregano, thyme, rosemary and others for which we commonly use the term "herb", but are used to flavour our recipes in the same way as "spices" are.

▶ Exceptions to the Rule

There are several plants foods included in the book that do not neatly fit this definition. They are green tea, soy and citrus.

In the case of green tea, although it is a beverage, the amounts that are consumed by an individual are very small – about the same quantities one would consume if it were a spice. Soy, although primarily a staple food crop, is also used in the common condiments soy sauce, tamari and others. The skins of citrus fruits are used as the food flavouring known as "zest", and it is this part of the plant that contains many of its most important phytochemicals.

Another reason that these three foods have been included is that they contain some of the most thoroughly researched phytochemicals that have been shown to protect humans against several important degenerative conditions.

▶ Scientific Evidence

There are several different types of research that can be used to show whether or not a specific spice or phytochemical contains therapeutic properties.

- *Epidemiological studies* are usually the first indicators that show whether or not a particular population group derives any health benefits from the consumption of greater than normal quantities of a specific spice.
- *in vitro* (laboratory) research is another way in which scientists look at the behaviour of spice-derived phytochemicals and their effect on human cells and biological processes.
- *Animal studies* are usually the next step where animal models, that closely resemble human pathological processes, are used to determine if the spice or phytochemical does indeed work to prevent or treat a specific disease.
- *Human clinical trials*: Neither the results obtained from the *in vitro* studies nor those derived from the animal models can be fully extrapolated to the human condition but are usually steps that must be taken before human tests can be done. Human clinical trials are the last stage in the sequence of tests used to determine if a specific modality is an effective *treatment* or not, and a well designed "double blind" clinical trial is considered the "gold standard" in this respect. Clinical trials to show whether or not that same substance could *prevent* the disease from occurring in the first place are somewhat more difficult to do; they usually need a longer time span before the results become apparent and also require a much larger cohort of participants to ensure that the results will be statistically significant.

For these reasons, although positive epidemiological results are commonly based on the *preventive* characteristics of spices, most of the *in vitro*, animal and human studies have looked at the *therapeutic* properties of the whole spice or its constituent phytochemicals. Therefore an assumption has been made that, if the epidemiological evidence shows that a spice has protective effects, the subsequent laboratory and clinical studies that demonstrate therapeutic properties are confirmation of its prophylactic characteristics.

15

Not many phytochemicals have been researched to the point of the clinical trial, hence much of the evidence presented here is based on epidemiological, *in vitro* and animal studies.

❱ Scientific Terminology

Scientific concepts often require the use of specific scientific terminology, and these terms are explained as new concepts are introduced. However, there is also a glossary at the end of the book that can be referred to.

❱ Why Not All Spices Have Been Included

Although most of the well-known spices have been included in this book, there are readers who will notice that some are missing. In order to justify their inclusion in the book, only those commonly used spices that show a degree of scientific evidence to back up their claims of having prophylactic or curative properties have been selected. Those that have been excluded may indeed have great health benefits and, at some future date, could become the targets of intensive research.

❱ Further Information

As more information becomes available it will be posted on the website: www.medicinalseasonings.com

Reasoning for Seasoning CHAPTER 2

▶ Macro- and Micronutrients

As modern medical and nutritional research has progressed over the past century, more nutrients and their physiological roles have become identified. Today we can say with such certainty which macro- and micronutrients the body needs to survive that we can keep mammalian cells alive in the laboratory for long periods on a scientifically formulated nutrient broth.

However, there are still disagreements about dosages, minimum daily requirements and the use of nutrients to *treat* diseases rather than their primary role, which is to maintain optimum biochemical homeostasis. A recent study in Baltimore, USA, showed that there is *no* statistically significant association between dietary vitamin C, vitamin E, and beta-carotene intake, and mortality from cardiovascular disease and cancer. However, the same study found that a greater than normal intake of *fruit and vegetables* was associated with *lower* risk of these groups of diseases. Fruit and vegetables contain vitamins C, E and beta-carotene in abundance, and yet supplementation of these nutrients on their own does not appear to confer the same protection as the plants that provide more than adequate amounts of them. Of the many studies done to date, there is very little compelling evidence to show that, in those individuals on an otherwise balanced diet, taking *extra* vitamins and other nutrients confers significant protection against cancer, heart disease and other degenerative diseases.

▶ Epidemiology

In spite of the apparently adequate intake of most of the well-recognised nutrients amongst most people in affluent countries, there is a spiralling increase in the incidence of most chronic diseases: namely cancers, heart disease, diabetes, arthritis and neurodegenerative diseases such as Alzheimer's disease. Some attribute this to the fact that we live longer than we used to, but this argument falls away when we look at some affluent (especially Eastern) countries that have very high average longevities and lower incidences of chronic degenerative diseases. Even some developing nations have lower incidences of these diseases in spite of many of their citizens living in conditions that are conducive to the development of the same chronic diseases. For instance lifestyle habits, like smoking tobacco, are considered responsible for some common cancers of the industrialized world.

An interesting piece of data, however, concerns the relationship between smoking and cancer in Thailand. Almost 50 percent of Thai males smoke, and most of them start the habit before they are 14 years old. The smoking rate there has been high since the middle of last century, so we have a long time-span to compare the impact of smoking on their health to that of other cultures. The incidence of lung cancer in the United States for males is 62 per 100,000 persons, while in Thailand it is only 25 per 100,000. The Thai people also have an average lifespan that is close to that of the US and therefore live long enough for this type of cancer to potentially predominate in their society. It makes sense, therefore, to look at the types of food that Thais and other nationalities eat to see if there are additional protective factors in their diets.

▶ The Mediterranean Diet

Over the past decade or so much has been made of the so-called Mediterranean Diet. Epidemiological evidence has shown us that people living in some Mediterranean countries of Europe have a lower incidence of heart disease relative to the USA, UK and some other European nations. Various hypotheses have been put forward as to why their diets should afford protection against heart disease and other degenerative conditions. The people of this region, when following their traditional diets, tend to eat less animal-derived saturated fats and more plant-based unsaturated fats (especially those found in olive oil) than most other

Western societies. In addition they eat less meat and more fish, vegetables, whole grains, legumes and fruit than their less healthy neighbours. These are all important dietary factors that are now being promoted by the medical profession and governments of countries like the USA that have particularly high incidences of heart disease. However, there are other factors that contribute to the favourable health status of those societies that adhere to the features typifying a Mediterranean-type diet.

Red wine has high levels of important antioxidants that have been shown to help in reducing the amount of arterial damage caused by a diet high in saturated fat; the fact that some Mediterranean countries boast very high levels of red wine consumption has been put forward by some scientists as the reason for this difference. Several studies show that the phytochemicals in red wine, especially resveratrol, do have powerful cardioprotective effects. Other researchers have pointed out that olive oil is also consumed in large quantities in this region and, although it is well accepted that this and other monounsaturated oils do protect against cardiovascular disease, recent analysis of extra virgin olive oil has shown that it also contains significant quantities of other phytochemicals like oleocanthal that have cardioprotective effects.

Other common foods in the cuisine of the Mediterranean basin are also thought to be protective against heart disease; therefore it is unwise to claim that any one substance is responsible for providing most or all of the cardiovascular protection for the people of this food-loving region. Although there are important protective chemicals in red wine and olive oil, what is often overlooked is the large variety of spices used on a daily basis in the recipes of this region. Large quantities of garlic, parsley, sage, rosemary, caraway, coriander, cumin and thyme are some of the staple spices that have been used for thousands of years (and still are) in many traditional Mediterranean dishes. As a group, these plant foods have properties that are probably similarly – if not more – effective at preventing cardiovascular and other diseases than red wine and olive oil.

▶ Obesity

Apart from lifestyle choices and pollution, much of the blame for the increase in chronic disease in the West has been laid on the increased consumption of calories (in the form of refined carbohydrates and animal fats) leading to excess weight and obesity. However, it is becoming clear that there are other important dietary factors that are influencing these alarming statistics. Some very recent research has shown that, although obesity is a serious global health problem, it has become somewhat fashionable to blame it for all manner of health problems. In some cases obesity is a condition *associated* with dietary factors (both deficiencies and excesses) that have led to the parallel increases in weight *and* the development of chronic diseases.

▶ The Need for More Phytochemicals in the Diet

As we have moved away from traditional diets, not only are we consuming unnecessary quantities of carbohydrate and fat, but the industrialisation of agriculture, harmful food-processing methods and our increasing reliance on convenience foods has led to a steady *exclusion* of many important foods from our diets. One of the dietary components that we are eating less and less of is plant fibre. It is well known that by refining foods and leaving out the fibre content of plants we have made ourselves susceptible to several diseases, including heart disease and diabetes.

Another group of substances occurs in various foods that we do not take enough of, and which are vital in the maintenance of health and the prevention of chronic disease. These are the biologically active compounds that occur in some of our lesser-used foods in the West. A new body of research is uncovering the role that common culinary herbs and spices play in the prevention of serious diseases. Some of the chemicals found in these plants have been identified and are now being tested as *treatments* for heart disease, diabetes, cancer, Alzheimer's disease and others. However, it is the *prophylactic* role of these herbs and spices and the phytochemicals they contain that present us with the most exciting opportunity to avoid the onset of our most lethal and costly diseases.

▶ Evidence

The pointer to the "medicinal" effects of culinary spices has been the increasing amount of epidemiological evidence showing that a particular population group eating large quantities of these foods has lower incidences of one or more disease entities. This has led scientists to try to identify the specific biologically active compounds in the plants concerned and then to measure their efficacy in laboratory, animal and human studies. At present there are many plants and their attendant phytochemicals under investigation by universities, governments and pharmaceutical companies for potential use as treatments for some of our most serious and prevalent illnesses. Notable amongst these are cinnamon for the treatment of diabetes and curcumin (an extract of turmeric) which has shown great promise as a novel therapy for cancer. Some companies have managed to synthesise chemicals similar to these natural extracts that they claim to be more effective in treating the disease than the original phytochemical.

▶ Keys to Disease Prevention

As exciting as the potential they show as individual, new treatments for modern maladies, it is the role of spices as unadulterated food components that help to prevent disease, where they show their greatest benefits. Well-known spices, fruits and vegetables such as garlic, rosemary, turmeric, cinnamon, ginger, black pepper, broccoli, citrus and many others contain phytochemicals that can prevent the onset of diabetes, cancers, heart disease and Alzheimer's disease. The quantity of these foods consumed varies, but generally, in the West, we do not use them often enough and in sufficient amounts to realise their potential as disease-preventing agents. To achieve optimum protection, we would have to alter our diets – and thus our palates – substantially to achieve the health benefits that only the greater daily consumption of spices will bring. Epidemiological evidence demonstrates that these spices need to be an integral part of our diet for them to be effective chemoprotective agents. For example, a typical adult living in India – where the very low rates of most cancers, heart disease and Alzheimer's disease have been attributed to high consumption of a variety of spices – consumes almost 10 grams of spices per day!

▶ Self-medicate with Spices

We must increase our intake of these products dramatically: it is not enough for us to have a curry meal once or twice a week and then a hot Mexican meal on the weekend. If we want to protect ourselves effectively, we must consume much larger quantities of culinary spices than most of us do at present. The average person on a typical Western diet probably consumes no more than a gram of spices a day – substantially less than the 10 grams that the average Indian adds to her daily meals. To reach this level we would either have to make radical dietary changes or take the spices in a pill or capsule form.

Modern research, epidemiology and, in retrospect, common sense and history are telling us that many of the most important therapeutic chemicals are found in the vast pharmacy contained within the numerous food types that mankind has been using for thousands of years. All foods have some health-providing properties, from those supplying us with the basic nutrients of carbohydrate, protein and fat, to those that provide us with vitamins and minerals. Still others play a very important protective function in the provision of antioxidants, antimutagenics, cholesterol-lowering agents and other important disease-preventing molecules. It is this last group of phytoprophylactic chemicals that are found in abundance in the foods that provide us with our most highly coloured and flavoured seasonings – those of the culinary spices and herbs that are to be found in many of the world's traditional cuisines.

All the evidence shows that our staple diet in the West is woefully short of some of the most powerful plant compounds that abound in the everyday diets of many other population groups. We must appreciate that we actually *need* these pungent foods to stay healthy – especially in later life – and we have to take them regularly, as the body benefits most when we provide it with a constant supply of a variety of plant-based chemicals. Spices are medicines, and in this context it is acceptable to be hypochondriacs and to self-medicate every day. For that is exactly what the spices contain – medicinal molecules that our physiological processes use to protect us from the ravages of the environment and the aging process.

▶ Shotgun versus Magic Bullet

Unlike the treatment of existing disease where we strive to find a "silver bullet" for each specific malady, in the case of preventive medicine we need to take the "shotgun" approach. Medical science is discovering more and more silver bullets that are used to treat various diseases. Antibiotics are probably the first modern medicines that could be classified as silver bullets – a specific infection can be cured by a specific antibiotic. Bang! And the offending bacteria are dead. Our modern medical arsenal provides us with other bullets that can cure a number of cancers, and there are certain vaccines that are used to target specific, established infections.

Interestingly, though, some of the most exciting new silver bullets still being researched are plant-based chemicals. Many of these substances have been isolated from spices and are showing great potential as treatments for specific disease entities. This is great news for all of us but, as the pharmaceutical laboratories are busy with the development of these products, we should not stand idly by. It takes years to develop new drugs, and they may only be available for general use long after some of us need them. It is vital for us, wherever possible, to take responsibility for preventing the onset of disease, and to do this we have to take the shotgun approach. How do we do that? The answer is that we have to take lots of plant-based "drugs" or phytochemicals in their natural state. We should take them with all of our meals. Whenever we put food in our mouths, a medicinal substance should be going in at the same time. Food and medicine – the one should become synonymous with the other, and we should enjoy and look forward to our medicinally loaded meals. If we don't like spicy foods, we can take a dietary supplement that contains the most important spices and in this way obtain their benefits without having to eat meals that are incompatible with our palates.

In whatever form you decide to take these wonderful foods, read on to discover the compelling "reasoning for seasoning".

.

The Evolution of Spices in our Diets   CHAPTER 3

SUMMARY • SUMMARY • SUMMARY

- ☐ Spices contain a huge range of phytochemicals that have proven health benefits. Humans have been medicating themselves with spices, often unwittingly, for thousands of years.
- ☐ Hunter-gatherer societies that roamed over many different biomes ate a vast range of these protective foods, especially during times of famine when they were often the only plant foods available.
- ☐ When agrarian societies developed, the strong flavours and colours of these piquant foods made them valuable additions to meals as they added flavour and colour to otherwise monotonous dishes.
- ☐ Spices were important early preservatives, and the same chemicals that protect food from spoilage have protected humans over the ages from infection, intestinal parasites and a range of other diseases.
- ☐ Because a wider variety of spices grow in warmer climates, they feature far more often and in greater quantities in the cuisines of the world's warmer countries compared with colder countries where, today, synthetic food additives are often used instead of spices.
- ☐ Societies that have traditionally consumed lots of spices continue to benefit from the protection that these foods provide against cancer, heart disease, diabetes and Alzheimer's disease.

▶ Introduction

There is indisputable scientific evidence that almost all spices contain chemicals that have profound health benefits, helping to protect the body from numerous illnesses and, in many cases, acting as effective treatments for established diseases. In addition, some of the chemicals found in spices can act as *adaptogens*, enhancing the body's physiological processes – and thereby physical and mental performance – and improving the general feeling of well-being. The remarkable properties of spices are best demonstrated when we compare the health status of communities that have differing levels of spice consumption. Unsurprisingly, most epidemiological investigations have focused on modern examples of the health benefits of spices. As a result, studies such as those showing the dramatically lower levels of lung cancer found in Thai smokers compared to those in the United States dominate the media coverage of the effects of spices on human health. Their impact on human health is not, however, an exclusively modern phenomenon. For millennia, just as the success or otherwise of societies has been influenced by the availability of foods providing the macronutrients – carbohydrate, fat and protein – so access to spices, and their incorporation into traditional cuisines, has had a profound effect on the health of different societies. The evolution of spices in our diets is a fascinating story that shows not only the significance of spices to the health of our forebears, but also explains why most people living in Western nations today consume a variety and quantity of spices well below those levels needed to achieve the comprehensive health effects this food group is capable of providing.

❱ Incidental Elixirs

Millennia ago, as humans roamed across the continents, they were forced to adapt to a wide range of climatic and other environmental conditions. As the geography and climate of their habitat varied so did the selection of foods available to them. This was determined primarily by the type and variety of plants growing in each particular biome and to a lesser extent by the number of animal species inhabiting those regions. Our hunter-gatherer forebears covered great distances and crossed many biomes in search of food. As a result, over the aeons before agrarian societies were formed, most humans consumed a wide variety of plant species, dependent to a certain extent on the broad geographical area they inhabited. Some of these plants – typically those which were later cultivated by agrarian societies – contained the basic macro- and micronutrients needed for survival (carbohydrates, fats, proteins, essential vitamins and minerals). Many of the pungent, stronger-tasting, and richly coloured plants also contained an array of non-nutritive compounds that helped to fight infection, enhanced physiological and homeostatic processes, and prevented the onset of chronic disease.

Today we know that the piquant flavours, strong smells and bright colours characteristic of spices are a hallmark of the important phytochemicals such plants contain. These compounds provide a range of health benefits for plants, animals and humans; plants use them to protect themselves against disease and insect attack, while in animals and humans they help to prevent infection, parasite infestation and a range of other pathological conditions. The resilience that characterizes many spice plants means that, during times of famine, pestilence and drought, these are often the last edible plants to survive. When taken on their own, many of them have overwhelmingly strong flavours and may be very unpleasant to eat. However, choice was not a luxury often bestowed on our forebears and unpalatable foods, in the absence of tastier alternatives, were frequently the only forms of nourishment available to them. This was a fortuitous dietary hardship and one which resulted in unwitting, but important, self-medication. The health benefits provided by these pungent plants (and the vast array of protective phytochemicals they contained) were amplified by the broad range of different species that was consumed as these nomadic peoples moved from one region to another. However, when agrarian communities began to form, the variety of plant species consumed by these societies decreased. They became dependent on a small selection of cultivated crops and a limited variety of wild plants that grew in their immediate surrounds. Over time the therapeutic benefits of some spice plants did become apparent, and these were incorporated into many folk-medicine pharmacopoeias.

Generally, however, the preventive health benefits derived from eating spices are, and always have been, an unconscious, albeit vitally important, act of self-medication.

❱ Functional Food Pharmacies

Intentional or incidental, the consumption of health-enhancing and disease-preventing chemicals found in spice plants is thought, at least in part, to have determined the health and thereby dominance of one tribe or larger community over its neighbours. In addition to the obvious menace of attack by other tribes or predatory animals, hunter-gatherer groups and later agrarian societies, lived under the constant threat of contracting lethal infections which could often develop from what we would consider innocuous wounds. Those of our forebears who survived into middle and old age then faced the threat of the same chronic diseases that plague us in the modern era.

Spices, many of which have powerful antimicrobial and anti-inflammatory properties, were invaluable to these early societies. In addition to their obvious association with acute conditions, infection and inflammation are now known to be the cause of a wide range of chronic illnesses. Not only are bacterial infections the cause of numerous acute life-threatening diseases, but those such as *Helicobacter pylori* are also responsible for chronic conditions like stomach ulcers. Similarly viruses are responsible for many acute infections like influenza but are also known to be the cause of chronic diseases such as cancers of the liver (hepatitis viruses) and cervix (human papilloma virus). Inflammation can result in acute and sometimes debilitating short-term pain, but it is also the underlying cause of many chronic degenerative diseases, such as arthritis, and it plays a fundamental role in the development of cardiovascular disease. While the causes, origins and broader implications of infection and inflammation are too numerous to discuss in detail here, it is interesting to examine one example that clearly illustrates their importance as pathological processes that underlie both acute and chronic diseases.

Periodontal infection is something that most of us would consider fairly innocuous. It is, however, increasingly believed to be a major cause of the chronic inflammation that underlies a range of serious chronic conditions. Untreated gingivitis, or even simple dental plaque, can be a reservoir for bacterial infections that stoke the fires of the chronic systemic inflammation known to underlie pathological processes associated with heart disease, cancer, autoimmune diseases and other illnesses. Modern methods of dental hygiene, such as flossing and brushing teeth regularly, are important tools in preventing these infections from occurring but, before the advent of these preventive strategies, our forebears had to rely on their natural environment to provide protection against, and treatment for, oral infections. This was not quite the poor alternative it might seem. Before the days of sophisticated food processing, people regularly chewed on plants with tough skins or fibrous flesh, and these provided the mechanical means to clean out the spaces between the teeth and remove infection-enhancing plaque.

In addition to the physical benefits derived from chewing these foods some substances, especially the spices, also acted as antiseptics. Most spices are potent microbiocides, the strongest of which contain chemicals that kill almost all the micro-organisms that they come into contact with. Some of them, such as mint, cinnamon and ginger, also help to reduce halitosis and ward off hunger pains, and are examples of spices that were regularly chewed by our forebears for the same reasons that we chew on flavoured chewing gum today. The regular mastication of these substances played a considerable role in helping to reduce potentially fatal infections that, in pre-dentistry days, were thought to have killed more people than most other causes of death. Once swallowed, most of these would also have provided protection against worms, other intestinal parasites and the same degenerative diseases that afflict modern man.

Many spices also improve physical endurance and mental agility. The members of those societies that had access to a range of these disease-preventing, adaptogenic foods would have been stronger, less prone to disease, and they would have been more effective hunters and warriors than their spice-deprived enemies. Their babies and children would have been healthier, had higher survival rates, and their communities would have been more resilient as a result. For these early societies, whether fighting for life against unforgiving environmental conditions, predatory animals or enemy tribes, the humble spice was often a powerful determinant of their success and population growth in a world when "survival of the fittest" was very much a reality.

▶ Spicy Satiating Snacks

As most of us have learned by experience, spices are delicious when used as seasonings, but few of them are considered much of a delicacy when consumed on their own - the form in which these foods were generally eaten by our hunter-gatherer ancestors. To most of us, even the thought of eating a ginger root, cinnamon bark, or chewing on a clove is thoroughly unpleasant, but for our ancestors this would not have been much of a hardship. As they were forced to eat them out of necessity, our forebears probably came to enjoy the intense flavour experience that many of these spicy plants provided. The major factor underlying the difference in tastes between modern and ancient societies, and between different cultures today, can be attributed simply to conditioning: when we are exposed to a food at a young age or for long enough period later on in life, we are more likely to acquire a liking for it. Many of us will have experienced this effect ourselves when, typically as adults, we initially find a novel taste or flavour unpleasant or even revolting. After subsequent exposure to the same food, we begin to find the taste inoffensive and maybe even delicious.

The second important factor that influenced the palatability of spices to our ancestors was the relative strength of flavours between different foods. To understand this, it is necessary to consider that most of the fruit and vegetable species eaten by early societies were stronger tasting and less sweet than they are today. In fact, the majority of modern plant-food cultivars bear very little resemblance to those varieties that grew thousands of years ago: the bitter, sour and astringent flavours that characterised fruits such as apples, melons, pears and many others have been bred out by generations of selective propagation. The cultivation of these species has also increased the sugar content of their fruits and reduced the amount of tangy chemicals that plants produce as defences against microbe and insect attack. In other words, our ancestors were far more accustomed to eating fruit and vegetables that had less sugar but sharper flavours than many of those that are available to us at present. Before the advent of crop cultivation and plant breeding, there was not as big a gap between the piquancy of fruits and vegetables and that of spice plants as there is today. Therefore our ancestors would have found it a lot easier to eat the "spicy" plants than we do now.

▶ First Food Flavourings

As hunter-gatherer peoples began to be replaced by agrarian societies, motives for the consumption of spices began to change. With the advent of crop cultivation, plant foods could be stockpiled and stored for use in times of scarcity, so these communities were less often forced to eat hardy spices as a last resort or as snacks "on the hoof" as their nomadic forebears had done. Instead, among more settled societies, spices became cherished as flavourings that could be used to augment the more monotonous diets that were based on a restricted number of cultivated crops. Strong-tasting spices could transform otherwise plain meals, and it was not long before the cooks of the day began to incorporate spice plants into what would become the traditional dishes of the world's emerging cuisines. Nor was it only dishes made from these foods that benefited from seasoning: spices were frequently used to increase the palatability of important but insipid animal proteins. Snails, for instance, which abound in the lush, green growth of temperate climates, were for thousands of years a valuable protein source for people who were unable to obtain tastier meat or fish protein. As anyone familiar with French cuisine knows, the addition of a little garlic and other spices can transform the unappetising flesh of the humble snail into a satisfying gastronomic experience – one that has stood the test of time and millions of cultured palates. All over the world, we find similar instances of other somewhat bland animal proteins that, with the help of a few simple spices, can be turned into gourmet treats.

❯ Colourful Cuisine

As food additives, spices were not just valuable flavourings. Many of them became prized as food colorants that could be used to dramatically enhance the appeal of the typically bland-looking foods derived from cultivated crops. In the natural world, where appearance and flavour often go hand in hand, our attraction to colourful foods is an instinctive reaction. Most fruits, for example, have deep or bright colours – orange citrus fruits, purple plums and berries, bright red apples, berries and mangoes, dark purple passion fruit, bright yellow bananas and many others. Humans and animals are initially attracted to a plant food by its colour; they are then rewarded by its flavour and return the favour by spreading the plant's seeds. Although in modern societies we no longer play the role of seed disseminators, the attraction to the colour of food persists. If we consider the rainbow of colours use in processed foods today, it is easy to understand how strongly visual appeal still influences the attractiveness of foods. Packaged foods have bright designs on their labels, sweets and beverages contain added colouring as do processed meats and dairy products. All of these are examples of how food manufacturers and vendors rely on aesthetics to attract people to their products.

Today, unfortunately, most of these visual effects are achieved with the help of synthetic pigments. In traditional Eastern and Mediterranean cooking, however, the addition of strongly coloured spices such as saffron, turmeric and paprika, or the adornment of food with the fresh green leaves of basil, parsley or mint remains an integral part of food preparation. The visual effects of these bright spices are equal to, if not better than, those provided by the synthetic alternatives, and natural colorants have numerous attendant health benefits. In plants, rich and bright colours, like strong flavours, are often produced by the powerful, protective phytochemicals such as flavonoids, polyphenols and carotenoids, that, when consumed regularly and in sufficient quantities, provide a wide range of health benefits.

❱ Powerful Preservatives

In order to establish food security, settled societies began to store the plants they grew or animals they killed, and food preservation became a priority. Here spices played two important roles. Their hardiness made them easy to cultivate and store, and many of them came from shrubs or trees that had uses beyond that of simply providing a food crop. The bay tree, for example, provides its leaf as a spice, its wood for furniture and the fruit of this tree was used for making soap. Secondly, and perhaps more importantly, spices could also act as preservatives and insect repellents for stored food.

The preservation of food had, to a certain degree, been a feature of our lives even before we adopted more settled lifestyles; like the San Bushmen still do today, hunter-gatherers dried some of the meat following a hunt and carried it with them as they moved from one encampment to another. When humans became more settled, they no longer needed to "travel light". Conversely, as they built permanent dwellings, planted crops and raised animals that needed tending, they lost the mobility to journey long distances to find nourishment. Other strategies were required to ensure a constant supply of food. The crops that they cultivated, the meat they obtained from their animal herds and the fish that they caught needed to be preserved to feed the larger populations that typified more sedentary societies. Drying of food was one solution, as was the use of the refrigerant effect of the low temperatures found at higher altitudes and latitudes. However, until recent times, the desiccation and freezing of food was not a viable option for that significant part of the world's population living in the hot, humid tropical and sup-tropical regions. In warmer climates, man was thus forced to become more innovative in his food storage techniques and discovered chemical preservation, in the form of salt and spices. As the former was only available in certain places (in the days before long-distance bulk transport), spices were often the only other option.

Scientists have now confirmed that many of the culinary spices typically used in warmer countries, have strong antimicrobial properties that assist in the preservation of meat or, when used during cooking, can kill microbes or neutralize toxins that have already contaminated the food. A number of familiar culinary plants show remarkable antimicrobial effects. The most potent of these include garlic, onion, allspice and oregano, followed by thyme, cinnamon, tarragon, cumin and capsicums (including chilies and other hot peppers). Black and white pepper are somewhat weaker microbiocides as are ginger, anise seed, celery seed and the juices of lemons and limes. Many of these spices kill or repel microbes and insects, and can be used to help protect stored food from decay and infestation. We now know, moreover, that many of the strongly flavoured phytochemicals which give plants protection against insect and microbial attack are the same chemicals that "preserve" our bodies, by protecting us against degenerative diseases and by slowing the aging process.

Spicy traditional recipes are more than proof of humans' long-standing visual and taste preferences; they are a historical record of the battle between us and the myriad organisms that compete with us for food. They have always been a significant weapon in this battle and, even in those instances when microbes caused slight food contamination, the strong flavours of spices could also be used to disguise the unpleasant effects of minor food spoilage.

▶ Seasonings in the Sun

We have seen that a combination of the flavouring, colorant and preservative qualities of the strong-tasting and brightly coloured plants we now refer to as spices served to perpetuate their use in the transition from hunter-gatherer times, when they were often consumed out of necessity, to the cuisines of sedentary societies, in which people could generally afford to be more selective about the foods they ate. Used to augment the flavour and colour of dishes, rather than as essential foods in themselves, people began to use spice plants in the form that they are used today – to enhance their recipes.

If we look at the somewhat bland fare that dominates the cuisine found in some countries and compare it to the recipes found in many others, it is interesting to see why spices feature prominently in the traditional cuisine of some cultures but to a far lesser extent in those of others. One of the most important factors in this respect is that of geography, so it is no surprise to find that spices are generally consumed in much greater quantity and variety in warm, humid countries (that also have the highest plant biodiversity) than in colder climates. When agrarian societies formed in the hotter regions, they had a wide range of spices available to them that could be incorporated into their cuisines. By contrast plant biodiversity is narrower in cold climates, and people who settled these localities were unable to access the variety of edible plant species that those dwelling in warmer climates were able to cultivate or gather from the wild.

Food in hot, humid climates spoils more easily than it does in colder regions therefore the people in the former used the preservative properties of spices as an added incentive for their use in cooking. Even the most cursory examination of the current relationship between climate and different countries' spice consumption supports the contention that spices are consumed in far greater quantities in hot rather than cold countries. India and Thailand have the highest production and consumption of spices; the warm Mediterranean countries follow somewhat behind these and other Eastern countries but are ahead of the United States. Lagging far behind are the chilly Scandinavian countries that have the lowest spice consumption of all. Moreover, the importance of spices in helping to prevent chronic degenerative disease can be seen to correspond to the varying levels of spice utilization that occurs across different temperature zones. The cold, low spice-consuming countries – also typically the most developed countries – tend to have much higher incidences of chronic degenerative diseases such as Alzheimer's disease, atherosclerosis, cancer and diabetes when compared to hotter, high spice-consuming populations. Importantly, this difference is significant even when other dietary and lifestyle factors like basic nourishment, smoking, drinking, environmental pollution and quality of medical services are taken into account.

▶ The Scourge of Synthetic Seasonings

Until fairly recently many spices were considered a luxury in those countries that were unable to grow them, while in their countries of origin even the poorest people used them as staple foodstuffs. Why, however, we might reasonably ask, with the development of long-distance transport of goods have societies that traditionally use few spices not increased their intake of these delicious foods? The obvious answer is that we like best what we are used to, but this does not fully explain the failure of the West to use more spices in processed foods and home cooking given that they have become cheap and readily available all over the world. One reason is that salt, which has for hundreds of years been an important feature of Western diets, is often considered to provide sufficient flavour enhancement. Sugar, too, has become one of the cheapest, most ubiquitous flavourings and is added to almost all processed foods. From a very young age our palates have become accustomed to foods that have a high sugar content, which tends to inhibit our appreciation of other flavours.

Another factor is the extensive use by the food industry of cheap artificial flavours and colourings that became available in the West over the last century. These artificial substitutes dramatically enhance the taste and visual appeal of foods in much the same way that spices have done for thousands of years. They also have the added advantage of being extremely cheap, and have been adopted with alacrity by the manufacturers of processed food, which now constitutes such a large part of our diets. Today synthetic food additives are ubiquitous and feature on the labels of almost all packaged foods. They have no health benefits, and it is unfortunate that they have prevented the wider acceptance of their natural, health-promoting counterparts that, since the advent of cheap cargo transport, have become affordable – if not quite as inexpensive as synthetic alternatives – and widely available the world over.

❯ Bon Appétit – Bonne Santé

The dearth of spices in the diets of those of us living in most Western countries means that we are depriving our bodies of the important phytochemicals that have, since time immemorial, been used by our physiological and homoeostatic mechanisms to provide us with an umbrella of protection against many diseases. Now that we are beginning to understand just how valuable they are to our health and well-being, we have no excuse for not regularly eating cinnamon (with its antidiabetic effects), basil (with its antiviral action), turmeric (with its powerful anticancer and anti-Alzheimer's disease effects), rosemary (with its cardioprotective action) and the scores of other spices that have these and many other health-promoting and disease-preventing properties. We need to consume a variety of spices on a daily basis as they can make us feel better, think better, age more slowly, and help us to resist the onslaught of scourges like cardiovascular disease, cancer, diabetes, Alzheimer's disease and other chronic degenerative disorders.

CHAPTER 4

Phytochemicals, Nutrients and Nutraceuticals

SUMMARY • SUMMARY • SUMMARY

☐ There are differences between the terms 'phytochemical', 'vitamin', 'nutraceutical', 'functional food' and 'adaptogen'.

☐ Vitamins and minerals are essential for normal physiological processes, while nutraceuticals provide extra protection against non-deficiency related diseases.

☐ Phytochemicals are a nutraceutical class of plant compound that exhibit protective or curative effects against disease.

☐ Macronutrients, like carbohydrates, fats and proteins, and micro-nutrients, like vitamins and minerals, are essential for the maintenance of health under normal conditions.

☐ Phytochemicals can help our bodies to maintain good health by enhancing biochemical processes and protecting us against toxins and other pathogenic processes.

☐ Malnutrition that results from the inadequate intake of dietary phytochemicals is common even among people who are not considered to be undernourished and increases the risk of developing chronic degenerative diseases.

☐ To ensure we obtain a sufficient quantity and variety of phyto-chemicals in our diets we need to dramatically increase our intake of phytochemical-rich foods like unrefined grains, fruit, vegetables and spices.

The remarkable disease-preventing properties of spices, that are the main focus of this book, are primarily attributable to what we may term "non-nutritive" phytochemicals or "*nutraceuticals*". Strictly speaking, all plant compounds are phytochemicals – including all plant-derived vitamins – but the primary task of this book is to focus on the nutraceutical phytochemicals provided by the spices. To this end, the following chapter outlines the differences and overlapping functions between these compounds and other nutrients, and explains the role each plays in enabling us to maintain good health.

Table 1: Nutrient Categorization

Phytochemical: In its broadest definition, a phytochemical is any plant-derived compound. As such it can include anything from plant macronutrients, plant-derived oils and vitamins to toxic substances that occur in poisonous plants. However, in the context of this book, the term is used to refer to those plant chemicals that are neither inert, toxic, nor essential nutrients like vitamins and minerals, but rather those that have protective and curative properties. For the purposes of this book a phytochemical is considered to be a nutraceutical.

Nutraceuticals: The word nutraceutical has been coined to describe non-essential, dietary substances – of either plant or animal origin – that have protective or curative properties. Nutraceuticals include that subset of phytochemicals that are the focus of this book.

Macronutrients: These compounds include carbohydrates, fats and proteins and are the nutrients needed by our body in substantial quantities. Their primary role is to supply the energy crucial for metabolism and to provide the basic building blocks for growth and repair.

Micronutrients: These are compounds, such as vitamins and minerals, that are required in much smaller quantities than macronutrients but are integral to numerous biochemical processes.

Vitamins: A vitamin is an organic molecule that is required by living organisms in minute amounts to sustain normal health. An organism deprived of all sources of a particular vitamin will eventually suffer from disease symptoms specific to that vitamin.

Minerals: These are elements such as *iron, calcium, magnesium, iodine, selenium* and *zinc* that are essential for the normal functioning of diverse biological processes.

Adaptogens: An adaptogen is a natural product that increases the body's resistance to stress.

Functional foods: These are foods containing molecules that have health benefits. As such, they could include almost all foods. By providing one or more vitamins, minerals, phytochemicals or macronutrients, most foods contribute to health. However, the term functional food is usually used to refer to foods that contain vitamins, minerals or nutraceuticals that have been shown to *provide health benefits for specific disease entities.*

To avoid confusion it is first necessary to clarify the differences in terminology used to describe the different classes of nutrients. Table 1 outlines those definitions most germane to the material discussed in subsequent chapters and, where relevant, specifies the way in which the terms are used in this book.

▶ Basic Health to Fortified Health

Although the health benefits of essential micronutrients and those of phytochemicals overlap to a certain extent, there is an important distinction between the two groups. Whereas vitamin and mineral micronutrients are essential for our survival and basic good health, phytochemicals take us beyond this minimum baseline, helping us maintain a state of health in the face of additional stresses, aging and pathogenic attacks on our bodies.

An inadequate intake of essential vitamins and minerals will, among other negative effects, lead to immune dysfunction and increase the risk of succumbing to infections and other diseases, in particular "deficiency" diseases such as anaemia, scurvy and pellagra. In very few cases however, vitamins or their analogues are being used to treat non-deficiency related diseases. Niacin (vitamin B3), for example is used in high doses to lower cholesterol, while the vitamin A analogue, Roaccutane, is an effective treatment for acne. However, there is no convincing evidence to show that vitamins – including vitamins E, C and ß-carotene – when taken in quantities exceeding the recommended daily doses, provide any additional protection against chronic degenerative diseases. Conversely, there is a substantial body of evidence to show that "non-essential" phytochemicals exhibit exceptional preventive and curative effects against diseases that are not related to vitamin and mineral deficiencies but include some of our most widespread and debilitating chronic illnesses.

Phytochemicals are not necessarily better than essential micro-nutrients; both are important, but in different ways. The maintenance of a country's stability – or health – provides a helpful analogy. Under normal conditions, a country has certain baseline requirements in order to run smoothly. These include, among others, a good government, a strong economy and an efficient police force and legal system. However, to deter external enemies and to protect itself in the event of attack, a country also needs a well-equipped defence force. In our bodies, macronutrients and essential micronutrients are the equivalent of the government, economy, judiciary and police, while medicines and nutraceutical phytochemicals correspond to the defence force. By protecting us against specific disease entities and enhancing processes integral to normal body function, phytochemicals fortify our bodies, enabling us to sustain a state of health in the face of attack by infections, toxins, cancer cells and other threats to our health.

▶ One Type of Fibre is not Necessarily as Good as the Other

We also need to be aware of inadvertently attributing the health giving properties of one dietary substance to another. A good example of this can be seen in the case of dietary fibre. Originally the term dietary fibre referred to the indigestible component of plant products, particularly those of the unrefined grains and legumes. Nowadays indigestible sugars (oligosaccharides) and starches (resistant starch) have been included in this category, and the properties attributed to the "original" high fibre foods like whole grains and bran are now being passed on to these "new" types of dietary fibre that do not contain the all important cell-wall components of the parent plant. Although the fibre itself does have several beneficial properties, there are other substances found in the cell walls of fibre-rich foods like whole grains that have important protective functions. Many of these are phenolic compounds and acids that have antioxidant and antimutagenic effects that have been shown to play a protective role against cancer. The "newer" fibre products, like indigestible sugars and resistant starches, do not contain these phyto-chemicals and it is probably unwise to think that taking them will provide the same degree of protection against cancer as those types of fibre that do provide these substances. Very recent evidence has shown that fibre *per se* does not protect against cancer of the colon even though it may protect against other diseases like heart disease and diabetes. This indicates that, rather than the fibre itself, it is actually the phytochemicals in the fibre-rich foods that are really providing protection against colon cancer.

▶ Modern Malnutrition

In wealthy countries, *under-nutrition*, resulting from inadequate calorific intake, is almost unknown. *Malnutrition*, however, is still a huge problem in the developed world. In this context, malnutrition is associated with two related factors. The first is excessive calorific intake, or *over-nutrition*, which has resulted in the obesity pandemic and a concomitant rise in obesity-associated health problems. The second is an increase in the incidence of degenerative diseases that, each decade, are occurring in younger age groups. Although lifestyle factors, such as a lack of exercise, play a role in these, a major contributing factor is a decrease in the quantity and variety of disease-preventing, health-enhancing phyto-chemicals in our diets.

During their production, refined foods, that comprise an ever increasing proportion of our diets, are stripped of many valuable nutrients. Increasingly, such foods are fortified with vitamins and minerals to replace those lost during processing, thereby providing the minimum quantities of nutrients needed to prevent the development of deficiency diseases. However, the valuable phytochemicals that are removed from our foods during processing are lost from our diets as they are not similarly replaced. The food-refining process not only discards the important fibre that occurs in many foods but, more importantly, deprives us of the protective phytochemicals that occur in the cell walls of fibre-rich plants.

If we are to benefit from the vital protective effects that phyto-chemicals are able to provide, most of us need to consume considerably more of these than we do at present. We can achieve this by eating more bread, cereals and other products made from unrefined grains and legumes, and by increasing our consumption of phytochemical-rich fruits, vegetables and spices.

In addition we can take a dietary supplement that will provide a diverse range of valuable phytochemicals. As spices are the most concentrated source of these, a daily dose of a good mixed-spice dietary supplement would provide a full complement of these vitally important compounds.

| CHAPTER | 5 | Safety Issues |

Safety Issues

SUMMARY • SUMMARY • SUMMARY

- ☐ Spices, taken in normal culinary quantities, have been demonstrated to be safe over thousands of years of use in many traditional cuisines.
- ☐ Spice-derived phytochemicals, like any other substances, can be toxic if consumed in very high doses, but they have a wide safety margin and generally only become toxic at levels far in excess of culinary quantities.
- ☐ Occasionally, spices may cause allergic reactions, but are no more likely to do so than other common foods.
- ☐ In moderate culinary amounts, spices are unlikely to pose a danger to pregnant women, children or people taking medicines.
- ☐ Spices do not contain any banned substances and can be taken by athletes.
- ☐ If there is any concern about a special risk factor, such as pregnancy, or if spices cause an adverse reaction, consult a medical practitioner.

▶ Tried and Tested

Not only are spices highly effective in protecting us against some of our most devastating diseases, they are also very safe. They can, for example, control blood sugar, blood pressure and cholesterol, and prevent and treat several specific diseases, but exhibit none of the unpleasant side effects associated with many of the drugs that are used to treat the same conditions. Their safety profile should come as no surprise to us as spices, being foods, have undergone a most comprehensive safety study: their place in many traditional cuisines has meant that they have been tested for thousands of years, by billions of people taking them on a daily basis. Their continued widespread use today is testament to the remarkable success of this unplanned, ongoing trial.

In evaluating the safety of a substance there are, however, two key factors to consider. The first is dose; the second is the possibility of risks associated with special circumstances of the individual, such as pregnancy, concurrent medications and age. In almost all cases, even in individuals with special circumstances, spices are safe provided they are taken in normal culinary quantities. However, as with all foods, there is always the possibility of exceptions to the rule, and this chapter explains the safety of spices in respect to dose and to each special risk factor, enabling individuals to make informed decisions pertaining to their individual situations.

▶ The Danger is in the Dose

Consumed in normal dietary quantities, spices are safe in all but exceptional circumstances. But like any substance, they can be toxic if they are taken in large enough amounts. There are numerous examples of this important principle – of too much of a good thing becoming a health hazard. For example, essential micronutrients like vitamin A can be extremely toxic in high doses; even excess calcium, which is required in relatively large quantities by the body, has been linked to an increased incidence of prostate cancer and kidney stones when consumed in excess.

The corollary of things being good in moderation but bad in excess, is that toxins, in small enough doses, are harmless. As the fifteenth century physician, Paracelsus, put it so elegantly:

"What is there that is not poison? All things are poison and nothing is without poison. It is solely the dose that determines whether or not a thing is a poison."

Indeed, some "toxins" are not only harmless in small quantities, but are actually beneficial. Such substances are said to exhibit hormesis. A substance showing hormesis is one that in a high dose inhibits (or is toxic to) a biological process, whereas in a much smaller dose will stimulate (or protect) that same process. A good example is the deadly toxin cyanide which is a minute constituent of the vitamin B12 molecule cyanocobalamine and other important molecules involved in our biochemical processes. Thus while a few chemicals present in vegetables, fruit or spices may exhibit toxicity if taken in large enough amounts, when they are consumed in normal culinary quantities, in the form of their parent plants, they are essentially harmless and usually beneficial.

▶ Optimum Dose and Safety Margin

When testing a chemical extract for use as a *treatment* for a specific disease, researchers establish the most effective therapeutic dose and the toxicity of that substance at various dosage levels. In order to derive the maximum benefits from spices, and to ensure that the quantities ingested remain within the safe and well established culinary parameters, we look to societies that incorporate large amounts of spices into their traditional cuisines. A person living in India, for example, eats an average of ten grams of spices every day. This figure provides a good target and upper threshold for spice consumption – a level at which spices exhibit their protective benefits but remain out of the danger zone. When determining the safe dose for a particular spice, the amounts used in spice-rich traditional dishes provide us with useful guidelines.

Because spices have a wide safety margin, it is acceptable to use the culinary-based quantities of spice consumption as a rule of thumb for estimating the doses we use to prevent the development of disease. Some substances, including many drugs, have a narrow margin of safety – where the therapeutic and toxic doses are very close to each other. Spices, on the other hand, have a very wide safety margin and there is a vast difference between their beneficial and toxic doses.

▶ Differences Between Medicinal and Culinary Spices

It is worth remembering that spices are commonly used *foods*, not drugs, and have been consumed daily for thousands of years by billions of people. There is generally a difference between a culinary herb or spice that is used for food enhancement and one that is used as a medication. Just as numerous plant extracts are used today as modern drugs so some culinary herbs and spices have been, and still are, used as therapeutic agents for specific diseases. Most medicinal herbs are not suitable for culinary purposes, but there is a degree of overlap between some dietary herbs and spices and those used in traditional medical systems. However, when a culinary spice is used as a medicine it is usually taken in greater quantities than when used as a flavour enhancer and often for only a limited period of time in those higher dosages. Ginger and garlic are good examples of two plants that have been used for aeons as both food flavourings and by traditional healers to treat a range of diseases. There are phytochemicals in garlic that when taken to excess are known to be both pro-oxidant and carcinogenic. This typically occurs when individuals take large quantities of garlic extracts and does not occur when it is taken in the quantities used in food – even in those recipes that call for large quantities of this spice.

▶ Extracts and Therapies

Many spices are being studied and used with a focus on their therapeutic rather than prophylactic action against disease. For therapeutic purposes, their constituent phytochemicals are often taken as concentrated extracts, or in amounts that far exceed culinary quantities. Higher, more concentrated doses may, in some instances, increase the therapeutic benefits, but they also increase the risk of adverse side effects. Concentrated extracts, such as essential oils, should therefore only be taken with caution and preferably under medical supervision. In general they should be used only to treat existing disease rather than for preventive purposes. The same care should be taken when taking whole spices in quantities well in excess of what one would normally consume as part of a spice-rich diet.

▶ Synergism

The other factor that frequently confounds our calculations is that of synergism. Many of the chemoprotective effects of phytochemicals are enhanced by the presence of other phytochemicals in the same plant or those found in other spices. One well-studied example of synergism involves genistein, an isoflavone found in soy. Genistein works synergistically with the bioflavonoids present in green tea and black pepper to enhance the bioavailability of curcumin, a valuable medicinal phytochemical present in turmeric. This has huge implications for the toxicity of these products as the more synergistic interactions there are between phytochemicals, the lower the dose of each individual spice required and the less the chance of side effects occurring. More and more of these synergistic relationships are being discovered and for that reason alone it is important to take as wide a range of spices as possible. It is more beneficial to consume a small amount of twenty different spices than a larger dose of one or two spice extracts. In this way synergism at the biochemical level will be enhanced and the possibility of side effects occurring reduced accordingly.

❱ Special Risk Factors

In certain circumstances, any substance taken in quantities that are normally considered safe may become a health risk. The following conditions are those in which this situation most frequently occurs.

☐ *Allergic reactions:* Unlike a side effect, which is an expected reaction based on a substance's chemical effects on the body, an allergy is an *abnormal* immune response to a substance. Just as a minority of people are allergic to common foods like peanuts, seafood and straw-berries, in rare cases, individuals may develop an allergy to any of the spices. Fortunately, as spices have many overlapping benefits and multiple functions, if one of them needs to be removed from the diet, there are others that can compensate. Both garlic and fenugreek, for instance, have potent lipid lowering effects; turmeric and rosemary help prevent Alzheimer's disease; and cinnamon and fenugreek lower blood sugar levels in diabetics.

☐ *Interactions with medicines*: Normal dietary components, including spices, rarely interfere with drugs and therapies or aggravate specific diseases. In fact, in the case of spices, the opposite effect is more often apparent. The phytochemical curcumin found in turmeric has, for instance, been shown to *enhance* the efficacy of chemotherapy and radiotherapy in the treatment of various cancers. If anything, those individuals on medication for chronic diseases would probably benefit from increasing their consumption of culinary spices. However, they should not do so without first consulting their physician as with a few drugs there are exceptions to this general rule. Grapefruit, for example, is an inhibitor of certain enzymes and interferes with the metabolism of the blood-thinning drug warfarin and it should be avoided by those taking this drug. There are, however, very few examples of spices interfering with the action of medicines.

☐ *Pregnancy and lactation*: To be completely safe, a highly spiced diet is not recommended during pregnancy, particularly during the first trimester, and all spices should be consumed in moderation during the remaining six months of pregnancy. During lactation, spices eaten by the mother can affect the taste of her milk and, in some cases, can cause colic in the breast-feeding infant. Lactating mothers should be aware of this and reduce the amount of spices in their diets if there are signs that they are affecting the baby.

☐ *Children*: Children under five years should only be given lightly spiced meals and these quantities can be increased as they grow older; children up to the age of fourteen may take amounts around half of those eaten by the average adult. Here again common sense should prevail and the traditional use of spices should be the guiding factor. Children also tend to let their taste buds regulate the quantities of spices that they are prepared to eat.

☐ *Athletes*: Spices do not contain any banned substances and athletes can benefit from their disease preventing, performance-enhancing properties without contravening any regulations. However, it is unwise to take massive quantities of spices in the hope that they will increase performance even further.

❱ Variety and Moderation

The best way to ensure that we derive the optimum health benefits of spices, without the risk of side effects, is to regularly eat a wide variety of them in normal culinary amounts. However, if there is a concern that they may pose a risk to an individual's health because of special circumstances (like pregnancy or concurrent medication) it is important to first consult a medical practitioner. Equally, if one suspects that an adverse reaction is caused by a spice then it should be removed from the diet or the quantity reduced in order to ascertain if it is indeed responsible for that reaction. It is worth bearing in mind that more is not necessarily better; it is important not to substitute a staple food with large quantities of a spice in the hope that it will produce even greater medicinal benefits. Instead, it is better to augment the diet with many different spices, in quantities which have been tried and tested over centuries of culinary use. In this way the myriad protective benefits of spice-derived phytochemicals reduce the chances of our developing some of the most dangerous illnesses, including cancer, cardiovascular disease, diabetes and Alzheimer's disease.

PART 2

HOW SPICES INHIBIT DISEASE PROCESSES

Mechanisms of Action CHAPTER **6**

S U M M A R Y • S U M M A R Y • S U M M A R Y

☐ By acting through a number of different mechanisms, the phyto-chemicals found in spices prevent and reverse many of the processes which underlie chronic diseases.

☐ Most chronic diseases involve several different processes, and spices frequently defend our bodies against specific diseases by counteracting more than one of these pathological mechanisms.

☐ The most important properties of phytochemicals include their role as antioxidants, anticarcinogens, blood lipid modulators, blood-thinning agents, blood sugar regulators, anti-inflammatory agents, antimicrobial agents, toxin neutralizers, bioavailability enhancers, synergistic compounds and as triggers for gene activation.

☐ These properties make spices effective preventive and therapeutic agents against some of the most serious chronic diseases, including cancer, heart disease, diabetes and Alzheimer's disease.

Underlying the development and manifestation of all degenerative disorders are a variety of pathological processes. Some diseases are already well understood and, as scientists learn more about both normal and aberrant biological mechanisms, further pieces of this vast puzzle fall into place. However, in most instances some processes remain unresolved while in others, such as Alzheimer's disease, even less is known about the underlying pathological mechanisms.

Our understanding of how a preventive or therapeutic substance works depends heavily on our knowledge of the pathological processes responsible for the disease in question. This applies both to the action of conventional drugs and to those of plant compounds. Sometimes we have a very clear idea of *how* a particular substance acts on a specific disease process. In other situations, although we know that a compound does indeed influence a process, we have yet to establish how it achieves this action. Often we know only that it has a measurable effect on the symptoms of the disease, without having any idea of the mechanisms involved. Chronic degenerative diseases, that are the most serious health problems in the Western world, are also some of the most challenging to elucidate. Many of these are the manifestation of several different and insidious underlying problems and are associated – directly or indirectly – with a number of lifestyle habits.

Atherosclerosis, which involves the narrowing and hardening of the arteries, provides a good example of the complexity that is a feature of most chronic diseases. It is caused by the deposition of cholesterol in the endothelial lining of the arteries, and we know that high blood lipid levels aggravate this process. However, raised blood lipid levels are not the only reason why atherosclerosis develops. Chronic systemic inflammation also damages the arterial lining and aggravates the atherosclerotic process. Blood platelets, which are responsible for thrombus formation, may also be a causative factor if they become "sticky". In this state they may aggregate to form clots in the coronary, cerebral, or other arteries, leading to heart attacks and strokes.

The complexity of the mechanisms underlying atherosclerosis and other chronic diseases means that there are a number of processes that can influence the progression and severity of these diseases. It also means that there are several areas towards which prophylactic and therapeutic interventions may be directed. In the case of atherosclerosis there are modern drugs that block at least two pathological processes: for example, statins lower blood lipids and aspirin reduces platelet aggregation. Similarly *cinnamon* and *fenugreek* lower blood lipids while *ginger, garlic* and several other spices reduce platelet aggregation. Several modern treatment modalities have been developed directly as a result of first understanding the underlying disease process, followed by the creation of a treatment that interferes with the whole, or part, of that process. A good example of this is tamoxifen which was developed specifically to deal with hormone-dependent breast cancers. Although we know how some spice-derived compounds work, more research is needed to determine precisely how many others function at molecular level.

This chapter examines the various preventive and therapeutic mechanisms through which several of these plant compounds have been shown to act, but a more detailed description may also be found in the chapters devoted to specific diseases. Where pathological processes are common to a range of diseases, this is pointed out. If a phytochemical has been shown to act on one disease by working though a particular mechanism, it is highly likely it will protect against other diseases with similar processes, even if these effects have yet to be studied.

▶ Antioxidants

An antioxidant is a substance which, by being oxidised itself, protects other chemicals and substances from oxidation. Antioxidants play a vital role in our bodies by limiting the damaging effects of the oxidative processes that have been implicated in the development of most degenerative disorders and the acceleration of the ageing process.

Oxidation is caused and perpetuated by free radicals. The unpaired electron common to all free radicals makes these molecules highly reactive and causes them to oxidise other substances, stealing an electron from their oxidative target in order to stabilise themselves. These targets are many and varied: DNA, cells, proteins, fats, and other molecules are all vulnerable to oxidative attack. Unless free radicals are intercepted by antioxidants the targeted molecules become free radicals themselves. This results in the development of a highly damaging "oxidative cascade" that continues to produce more and more free radicals and leads to an unhealthy condition called "oxidative stress". However, below a certain threshold, free radicals are not toxic and, in some cases, are in fact essential as they are harnessed by the body to destroy microbes and abnormal cells.

The body manufactures some of its own antioxidants, but in order to avoid oxidative stress these need to be supplemented through the diet. Spices offer one of the richest sources of antioxidants, with *allspice, cinnamon, clove, garlic, ginger, lemon balm, oregano, peppermint, sage* and *thyme* being especially potent. They also contain a particularly wide

55

Table 2: Key Medicinal Properties of Spices

Antioxidant (see chapters on antioxidants, salicylates)	Allspice, cinnamon, clove, garlic, ginger, lemon balm, oregano, peppermint, sage, thyme (Although all spices contain antioxidants, the above spices are the richest sources of these vital compounds.)
Anticancer (see cancer chapter)	Anise, basil, black pepper, caraway, citrus, cloves, fennel, garlic, ginger, green tea, mustard, rosemary, soy, turmeric
Blood Lipid Control (see cardiovascular chapter)	Caper, cinnamon, citrus, coriander, fenugreek, garlic, ginger, grape, oregano, rosemary, soy, star anise, thyme
Blood Thinning (see cardiovascular chapter)	Caper, cinnamon, coriander, fenugreek, garlic, ginger
Blood Sugar Control (see diabetes chapter)	Cloves, ginger, onion, oregano, rosemary, thyme
Anti-inflammatory (see inflammatory disorders chapter)	Bay leaf, black pepper, garlic, ginger, green tea, oregano, rosemary, thyme, turmeric
Antimicrobial	Allspice, anise seed, basil, bay leaf, black pepper, capsicum, cardamom, celery seed, cinnamon, clove, coriander, cumin, dill, fennel, garlic, ginger, lemon grass, marjoram, mint, mustard, nutmeg, onion, oregano, parsley, rosemary, sage, tarragon, thyme
Immunomodulation	Black pepper, garlic
Toxin neutralisation	Caraway, citrus, coriander, garlic, green tea, mustard, rosemary, turmeric
Bioavailability Enhancement	Black pepper
Synergism	Phytochemicals in all spices

variety of antioxidants which makes them effective at fighting many different kinds of free radicals, in different parts of the body. By consuming these plant foods, we can effectively fortify ourselves against pollution, smoking, excessive exercise, sunlight and a variety of other external factors that inflict a relentless free-radical assault upon us.

For further details refer to Antioxidants, page 69.

❱ Anti cancer Properties

Cancer is caused by a number of different factors, and a variety of pathological processes are involved in both its development and progression. Anticancer agents are substances which prevent or counteract cancer and work either by protecting the body against carcinogenic substances that trigger the disease or by modulating and suppressing the cancerous mechanisms themselves.

One of the most important roles of anticancer agents is to prevent, contain or repair DNA damage, which is the first step towards developing a malignancy. If the biochemical processes fail to repair damaged DNA or to destroy the cells in which it is contained, the cells' growth-control mechanisms may become ineffective. This leads to the unchecked proliferation of abnormal, pre-malignant cells, and ultimately to tumour formation. Preventing DNA damage is an ongoing battle as our bodies are constantly assaulted with carcinogens. These come from diverse sources including environmental toxins, petrochemicals, tobacco, alcohol, viral infections, sunlight, chronic inflammation and malfunctioning processes inside our own bodies.

Several spices protect against cancer by working at the crucial DNA level of tumourigenesis. They usually act in either of two ways. One of these is to protect DNA against oxidation by free radicals (many carcinogens are free radicals and vice versa). If unimpeded, free radicals can cause considerable damage to DNA and the numerous antioxidants found in spices play a crucial protective role by "mopping up" excess free radicals, thereby intercepting the first, pivotal stage in the development of cancer. The second way in which phytochemicals prevent injury

57

to DNA is by helping the body to neutralise or excrete the wide range of carcinogenic substances that have the potential to cause this type of damage.

The remarkable anti-tumourigenic properties of spices extend well beyond DNA protection. Spices contain compounds that fight cancer at each stage of its development and progression. They do this through a variety of mechanisms which include the inhibition of cancer-associated inflammation, the induction of cell death in malignant cells, direct attacks on tumours and the inhibition of tumour blood supply. In addition they can enhance radiotherapy and chemotherapy treatments for some established cancers. Many spices have anticancer properties but among the most important of these are *anise, basil, black pepper, caraway, citrus, clove, fennel, garlic, ginger, green tea, mustard, rosemary, soy* and *turmeric*.

For further details refer to Cancer chapter, page 75.

▶ Blood Lipid Control

Elevated levels of the blood lipids cholesterol and triglyceride are one of the most important risk factors for cardiovascular disease. If their blood concentrations exceed a certain threshold, these lipids, together with other substances, are deposited in the endothelial lining of the arteries. Eventually, sufficient quantities accumulate to form atheromatous plaques. These plaques contribute to the gradual narrowing and hardening of the arteries that characterises atherosclerosis, a disease which is ultimately responsible for most heart attacks and strokes.

Lowering blood lipid levels and preventing their deposition in the arteries is one of the most effective ways to reduce the risk of cardio-vascular disease. Spices contain phytochemicals that are effective in all respects. *Coriander, cinnamon* and *fenugreek*, for example, all reduce the levels of the carrier proteins that take cholesterol to be deposited in the arteries. *Ginger, oregano* and others protect against the oxidation of cholesterol that causes atheromatous plaque formation. *Bay leaf, garlic* and *turmeric* are all strong anti-inflammatory agents which can reduce the inflammation associated with the formation and enlargement of these plaques.

For further details refer to the Cardiovascular Disease chapter, page 84.

❱ Blood Thinning

Clot formation is an essential process, but if blood clots too readily it becomes a serious health risk with the potential to cause heart attacks or thrombotic strokes. Small blood cells called platelets play a crucial role in the formation of blood clots, however if these become "sticky" they become a potential liability, adhering to one another even when there is no bleeding. If this abnormal aggregation involves a significant number of platelets, a clot may develop. Sticky platelets also increase the risk of clot formation on an atheromatous plaque that has ruptured into the lumen of a blood vessel. A number of spices protect against heart attack and stroke by reducing the stickiness of platelets and "thinning the blood", thereby decreasing the likelihood of inappropriate clot formation. *Clove, garlic, ginger, oregano, rosemary* and *thyme* are all effective blood thinners.

For further details refer to the Cardiovascular Disease chapter, page 84.

❱ Blood Sugar Control

Ingested carbohydrates are first metabolised before being absorbed through the intestinal wall after which they cause a rise in blood glucose levels. These levels must be maintained within a fairly narrow margin and are prevented from rising too high by the release of insulin. Insulin is a hormone produced by the pancreas that stimulates cells to absorb glucose. Blood glucose is prevented from dropping too low by the reduction in insulin production that follows a fall in blood glucose concentration.

The disruption of the finely tuned blood glucose control mechanism can have dire consequences and is directly responsible for several diseases. Type I and Type II diabetes and metabolic syndrome are all caused by the body's inability to control blood glucose levels, either because of insufficient insulin or because cells become resistant to the effects of insulin. Acting through a variety of mechanisms, spices can augment or even replace the conventional treatments for diabetes and help to prevent both it and metabolic syndrome. *Caper, cinnamon, fenugreek* and *ginger* increase insulin sensitivity, while *coriander* enhances insulin secretion. *Fenugreek* modulates glucose absorption in the intestine and also lowers blood lipids. *Cinnamon* likewise lowers blood lipids as well as reducing oxidative stress caused by fat oxidation.

For further details refer to the Diabetes chapter, page 93.

❱ Anti-inflammatory Disorders

Inflammation is the immune system's response to infection, injury and chemical or physical irritation and is an essential component of many biological processes. Unfortunately, in addition to its beneficial effects, inflammation may have adverse consequences leading to allergies, autoimmune disorders and the destruction of healthy cells. Chronic systemic inflammation (CSI) is another manifestation of the potentially damaging effects of inappropriate inflammation.

CSI is a low grade, pervasive form of inflammation that has recently been implicated in a range of chronic degenerative diseases. While the biochemical processes are similar to those underlying acute localised inflammation, CSI is not restricted to a specific area of the body but involves the endothelial lining of blood vessels and many other tissues and organs. Diseases associated with CSI include metabolic syndrome, diabetes, and atherosclerosis, as well as some forms of depression and sleep disorders.

The phytochemicals found in spices have several ways in which they exert their potent anti-inflammatory properties. Some of them, such as *turmeric, ginger* and *bay leaf*, reduce inflammation by interfering directly with the inflammatory processes. Others, including *black pepper, garlic* and *green tea*, act as immunomodulators and help to control the excessive production of pro-inflammatory chemical messengers. The numerous antioxidants found in spices also help to limit the oxidation of lipids which is associated with inflammatory damage. Phyto-chemicals can also help the body to excrete a range of toxins that can trigger inflammation.

For further details refer to chapter 14, page 115.

▶ Immunomodulation

An immunomodulator is a substance that has a balancing effect on the immune system – reining in the overactive components and stimulating the weaker arms of the system. The immune system is a complex web of cells, chemical messengers and antibodies that protects against infection, environmental pollutants and those aberrant cells that threaten to develop into cancer cells. Normal physiological processes cannot work effectively without a healthy immune system; if it malfunctions we become vulnerable to infection, malignancies and toxins.

The immune system may become unstable and either attack the body's healthy tissues or overreact to substances from the environment. The former occurs in the autoimmune disorders like rheumatoid arthritis, lupus and ankylosing spondylitis. The latter abnormality manifests itself in the form of allergies; these can vary from milder allergies like eczema and hay fever, to life-threatening anaphylaxis, brought on by exposure to common foods such as peanuts and strawberries.

Allergies and autoimmune disorders occur when an imbalance between different sectors of the immune system results in an inappropriate immune response to normal tissues or harmless substances like food molecules. Antibodies may attack normal, healthy cells as well as stimulating certain cells to release abnormal quantities of different chemicals. In the case of allergies, substances such as histamine cause the symptoms of the allergic reaction. Autoimmune disorders are characterised by abnormal cytokine (chemical messenger) production that leads to an attack on normal tissue by the immune system's cells and antibodies.

A number of phytochemicals are powerful immunomodulators and are very useful in the prevention and treatment of the allergies, autoimmune disorders and weakened immune systems that can result from diseases such as HIV/AIDS. *Phytosterols*, compounds that are found in several spices and other food plants, are particularly effective in this respect and are currently being used to treat a variety of diseases like hay-fever, HIV/AIDS and hepatitis. In addition to supporting the immune system in its fight against external pathogens, immuno-modulating phytochemicals help to ward off autoimmune disorders by balancing and strengthening the immune system. Spices particularly rich in immunomodulating phytochemicals are *black pepper* and *garlic*.

▶ Antimicrobial Properties

Spices are some of the world's hardiest plants, containing a range of powerful phytochemicals that protect them from microbial and insect attack. Many of these same chemicals also confer on spices strong food preservation properties, enabling them to act against the microbes that cause food spoilage and food-borne diseases. These chemicals are likewise responsible for the remarkable antimicrobial effects of spices in our bodies.

Almost all of the commonly used culinary spices show some anti-microbial properties. *Clove, anise seed, thyme* and *allspice*, for example, are very effective in inhibiting the growth and toxin production of several pathogenic fungi. The fungi which these spices act against include those of the *Aspergillus* genus that produce the potent liver toxins responsible for certain types of liver cancer. A few examples of spices with strong antimicrobial properties are *garlic, allspice, oregano, thyme, cinnamon, cumin, capsicum, clove, rosemary, marjoram, mustard, mint, coriander, dill, parsley, cardamom, black pepper, ginger* and *anise seed*.

Although spices and their extracts have yet to be regularly used as antibiotics or antiparasitics, the rising tide of antibiotic resistance amongst some of the world's deadliest organisms is stimulating a growing interest in their antimicrobial properties. Medicinal honey, for instance, is effective primarily because of the many microbiocidal phyto-chemicals that it contains. These compounds are derived from the nectar of the various plants that bees collect to make honey. It is being used to prevent and treat the deadly methicillin-resistant staphylococcal infections that plague hospitals and claim the lives of thousands of post-operative patients every year. Phytochemicals act against many different microbes, and by consuming a variety spices we can fortify ourselves against an array of bacterial and viral pathogens.

▶ Bioavailability Enhancement

The bioavailability of a substance is the rate and extent to which it is absorbed unchanged and, ultimately, made available at sites of action in the body. If we can enhance the bioavailability of a molecule, we increase its efficiency and do not need to ingest as much as we would otherwise require. Bioavailability can vary from person to person, and changes with time and circumstance. Therefore although we may eat what we assume are the optimum dosages of a drug, herb or nutrient, this amount is not necessarily utilised with maximum efficacy by our bodies.

A substance's bioavailability can be reduced for a number of reasons. From the moment we put it in our mouths, several different factors begin influencing its absorption and metabolism. Sometimes the substance is altered by stomach acid and other chemicals in the intestine; its absorption may also be inhibited by enzymes that occur in the cells lining the small intestine. Once in the blood stream, it is taken to the liver, where a range of other enzymes can either retard or accelerate its metabolic breakdown. A well-known example of the factors that can influence the absorption – and thereby bioavailability – of a substance concerns the essential nutrient, iron. On average we absorb only about 20 percent of the iron that is present in our food. However this absorption can be either enhanced by the ingestion of vitamin C, or inhibited by drinking tea. If you are anaemic as a result of iron deficiency, you need to take your iron supplements with vitamin C which will enhance its absorption and hence its bioavailability. If, on the other hand, you have haemochromatosis, a disease that is caused by excess iron, then you should drink tea with your meals as phytochemicals in tea inhibit the absorption, and so the bioavailability, of iron.

Enzymes belonging to a class called cytochrome P450 are particularly important factors influencing bioavailability. Occurring in the cells of the small intestine and liver, these enzymes play a crucial role in the metabolism of at least 50 percent of administered drugs and ingested phytochemicals. Their activity varies considerably between different people: in the intestines this varies by up to 30 fold while in the liver there can be a 100 fold difference in activity between individuals. The effects of these enzymes also tend to decline with age, although there is a broad range of activity even within people of the same age group. Many substances that enhance bioavailability act on the P450 enzymes. Grapefruit, for example, contains furanocoumarins that are potent inhibitors of some of the enzymes responsible for reducing the bio-availability of a number of drugs. Patients taking these drugs may be advised not to eat grapefruit as it can lead to dangerously high blood levels of the drug.

In the case of foods and nutrients, however, bioavailability enhancement is usually beneficial. Some spices are strong bioavailability enhancers, improving the absorption and uptake of a range of important compounds, including those derived from other spices. *Black pepper*, for instance, contains piperine which is of the most powerful bioavailability enhancing compounds. Piperine can improve the bioavailability of phytochemicals in turmeric and green tea by more than a 1000 percent. Taking black pepper in conjunction with other spices can therefore enhance the effects of a myriad other valuable phytochemicals. This is only one example of the dual benefits obtained by increasing the number of different spices in our diet. In general, when we diversify our spice consumption, we increase the range of protective chemicals in our diet, as well as bolstering our body's ability to use them to optimum effect.

▶ Synergism

There is a complex web of synergistic relationships between different phytochemicals, and between these compounds and modern therapies. Bioavailability enhancement is one way in which phytochemicals can improve the effectiveness of other substances – in this case by increasing the efficiency of their utililisation in the body. There are other synergistic relationships in which one phytochemical boosts or even unlocks the prophylactic or curative properties of another substance. Some of these relationships are understood, but many have still to be identified and elucidated. It is the yet unknown synergism between thousands of phytochemicals that can underlie the phenomenon whereby an "active ingredient" thought to be responsible for the medicinal properties of a plant proves less effective when taken in its isolated form.

Synergism means that if we are to reap the full prophylactic benefits of plants, the consumption of a wide array of phytochemicals in their natural state is of paramount importance. The effectiveness of preventive medicine depends primarily on the ability to avoid, or curtail at an early stage, the numerous pathological processes which underpin most diseases. We are many years away from a complete understanding of these processes, let alone elucidating the ways in which phytochemicals act against them. Until then, it is necessary to give the whole plant the benefit of the doubt; we must assume that the combination of phytochemicals – as well as the chemicals themselves – is responsible for the plant's preventive properties. Additionally, by eating a wide variety of foods rich in bioactive compounds, we can unlock the benefits of synergism that often exist between the phytochemicals present in different plants.

One well-studied example of synergism involves *genistein*, an isoflavone found in soy. Genistein works synergistically with the bioflavonoids of green tea and black pepper to enhance the bioavailability of curcumin, a valuable medicinal phytochemical present in turmeric. Genistein also acts synergistically with certain cancer drugs like tamoxifen and can augment the efficacy of radiation for breast and prostate cancers. Curcumin has similar effects to those of genistein in respect of its synergism with modern cancer treatments.

Another example relates to *ginger* and *Siamese ginger*, which come from the same plant family. Individually, both spices have well-known anti-inflammatory properties. However, a combination of these two plants is far more effective in suppressing the production of pro-inflammatory cytokine chemical messengers than is either spice when taken on its own. Phytochemicals found in almonds are also known to work synergistically with one another. Almond skin contains high levels of catechins and flavonols, both of which are powerful antioxidants in their own right. In addition, catechins and flavonols act synergistically with two other antioxidants, vitamins C and E, to protect against cholesterol oxidation. The list is long and diverse, but in every case it points to the importance of eating many different plants in order to benefit optimally from the myriad phytochemicals they contain.

▶ Toxin Neutralization and Excretion

Every day we are exposed to a number of toxins – from environmental pollutants to the cancer-causing chemicals found in certain foods, such as red meat. While the body has mechanisms to deal with a limited variety and quantity of toxins, it needs additional help to counter sustained levels of these substances. Phytochemicals can be extremely effective in augmenting the body's mechanisms for combating toxins, thereby reducing their pathogenic effects. Cooked red meat, for example, contains a chemical called PhIP that even when consumed in moderate excess becomes a powerful carcinogen. Members of the *brassica* family, such as *mustard, wassabi, broccoli* and *Brussels sprouts*, have a protective effect against this toxin. They work by enhancing the enzymatic breakdown of PhIP in the liver by more than 130 percent. Once it has been broken down in the liver, PhIP is no longer a threat to the body and is rapidly excreted in the urine. In addition to those found in brassicas, the phytochemicals in *caraway, citrus, garlic, green tea* and *rosemary* neutralise a whole range carcinogens and toxins that we are exposed to on a regular basis.

Chelation is one of the most important ways in which phytochemicals can assist the body in fighting toxins. Environmental pollutants, especially heavy metals like lead and mercury, can cause severe damage to the nervous system and other tissues. The body struggles to excrete these elements which may, as a result, become deposited in various tissues where they can cause serious health problems and even death. Chelating agents are chemicals which, by binding with the toxic molecules, make it easier for the body to excrete the targeted toxin. Two commonly used chelating drugs are EDTA and penicillamine. These can be used to rid the body of lead, copper, mercury and other toxins. Certain spices contain phytochemicals that are also very effective chelating agents. *Coriander* and *turmeric* are two of the most potent chelating spices and can help the body to eliminate, among others, the toxic metals mercury and lead.

▶ Gene Activation

All biochemical interactions in the body, including those that combat pathogenic processes, are ultimately controlled by genes. Genes are responsible for regulating the production of enzymes and other substances involved in the cell's biochemical processes, and gene activation is one of the important mechanisms through which phyto-chemicals can protect us against disease.

Genes work in a comparable manner to the different software programmes installed on computers. Once the software is switched on, it can be used to carry out the functions that it was designed for. Excel, for example, is used for spreadsheets and calculations while PowerPoint has totally different properties. In a similar way, one gene may control the production of insulin by the pancreatic cells while another regulates the amount of adrenaline produced by the adrenal glands. For a gene to have its particular effect it needs to be "switched on", and most of those genes vital to life are always in this active state. However, other genes do require outside assistance and the "switches" that are needed for their activation may be plant-based compounds. By consuming plants rich in a range of bioactive phytochemicals, we can provide our homeostatic mechanisms with the means to "wake up" a range of dormant genes which, once activated, can have powerful preventive and therapeutic effects. These plant compounds also have the ability to enhance the activity of genes that are already switched on but are not functioning at optimal levels.

Although relatively little is known about the precise way in which phytochemicals – or indeed any substances – activate genes, there is mounting evidence to show how they do fulfil this role. Directly or indirectly, gene activation mechanisms are likely to account for at least some of the preventive and therapeutic properties of phytochemicals discussed in this chapter.

With the sequencing of the human genome complete, we are unravelling more and more of these mysteries but we remain a long way off from a complete understanding of the myriad complex ways in which dietary chemicals interact with biological control processes.

▶ Silent Killers

Most degenerative diseases take a long time to develop and by the time they manifest themselves in ill health their underlying pathological features have been there for many years. A heart attack, for example, occurs as a result of the rupture of an atheromatous plaque that has taken years to develop. An individual may be completely unaware that he has atherosclerosis until the day he finds himself in hospital being treated for a heart attack. Similarly, diabetes, Alzheimer's disease and most cancers are all diseases that manifest themselves after long periods of incubation, often in apparently healthy people. In this sense they are silent killers, a "fifth column" of diseases working insidiously inside our bodies. Apart from trying to diagnose and treat them as early as possible, the only other way we can deal with these diseases is to prevent them from occurring in the first place. This we can do to a large degree by ensuring that we make the right lifestyle choices and avoid factors that are known to aggravate the development of these conditions. If we are conscientious enough, we can take measures to reverse some of the damage that has already taken place.

One of the most effective ways we can deal with these sinister processes before (or even after) they show themselves as fully fledged disease entities is to ensure that we take adequate daily quantities of spices and other phytochemical-containing foods and supplements.

Antioxidants

CHAPTER 7

SUMMARY • SUMMARY • SUMMARY

☐ An antioxidant is a substance that prevents oxidative damage by neutralising the highly reactive and destructive free-radical molecules.
☐ Some free radicals are needed by the body, but oxidative stress occurs when there are insufficient antioxidants available to "mop up" excess free radicals. Oxidative stress can be caused by infections, drugs, smoking, pollution, radiation, excessive exercise, psychological stress and obesity.
☐ Damage caused by oxidative stress has been implicated in a range of diseases including cancer, heart disease and diabetes.
☐ Some antioxidants are produced by the body, but these need to be supplemented by the antioxidants found in foods.
☐ It is more important to take a wide variety of antioxidants than large doses of a few antioxidants. The best way to do this is by regularly eating a variety of antioxidant-rich foods.
☐ Spices comprise the food group containing some of the most important antioxidants.
☐ The most antioxidant-rich spices are *allspice, cinnamon, clove, garlic, ginger, lemon balm, oregano, peppermint, sage* and *thyme*.

▶ Free Radicals and Oxidation

An **antioxidant** is a substance which, through being oxidised itself, protects other chemicals and substances from oxidation. As a result of this property, antioxidants provide protection against the often highly damaging oxidative processes in our bodies that are caused and perpetuated by **free radicals**. The unpaired electron common to all free radicals makes these molecules highly reactive and, in order to stabilise themselves, they steal electrons from other compounds. This in turn oxidises the targeted substances (e.g. proteins, fats and DNA) that are all vulnerable to oxidation. To make matters worse, an unchecked oxidative

69

process results in a cascade of free-radical production with consequent cellular and other tissue damage.

As a result of their destructive and persistent properties, free radicals can cause havoc in our bodies and they have been implicated in a wide range of diseases. Cancer, for example, can be triggered by free-radical damage to DNA. Heart disease can begin with free-radical attack on cholesterol carrier proteins which, in turn, leads to atherosclerosis.[1] Free-radical damage has also been linked to diabetes, Alzheimer's disease, inflammatory disorders and a number of other pathological processes.

Like most substances found naturally in the body, free radicals are toxic only when they exceed a certain threshold. In some circumstances, the body actually *needs* free radicals to fight infection, and there is evidence that too much of one type of antioxidant can be harmful if it eliminates all of a useful free-radical species. Typically, however, an excess – rather than a shortage – of free radicals is by far the greater problem facing our bodies. In addition to those produced during normal oxidative processes, a whole range of environmental factors result in our exposure to other free-radical species. Smoking, pollution, excessive exercise and sunlight are among the many external factors that inflict a steady assault of free radicals upon us and that make antioxidants such invaluable substances to include in our diets.

▶ Oxidative Stress: A Persistent Threat

If there are insufficient quantities of antioxidants to match the production of free radicals, then the body is said to be in a state of **oxidative stress**. In this state, unimpeded free radicals cause damage that can lead to inflammation, immune dysfunction, DNA damage and, ultimately, a range of degenerative diseases. Although most of us are not in a continuous state of oxidative stress, we generally experience this unhealthy condition on a regular basis as it can be precipitated by a wide

---

1 For further details on these cholesterol carrier proteins, known as LDLs, and atherosclerosis refer to Chapter 9.

Antioxidants: The Facts and the Fiction

Antioxidants are undoubtedly some of the most important chemicals used to protect biological systems, but they are also the subject of much hype and misinformation. In order to understand how these remarkable substances can be used to full effect it is important to understand how antioxidants really work. Some of the most common misconceptions surrounding antioxidants are as follows:

☐ **A "Powerful" Antioxidant?** Many health products almost claim to be panaceas because they contain large quantities of, what is claimed to be, a strong antioxidant. Often, this antioxidant is said to be "more powerful" or "stronger" than other antioxidants. The implication is, of course, that this product is all we need to provide ourselves with antioxidant protection. This is an incorrect and potentially damaging perception. Measured against laboratory standards, one antioxidant may indeed prove more effective – or powerful – than another, but this is only true under certain conditions. No one antioxidant neutralises all free-radical species no matter how potent that compound is, and that is the most important reason why we should not rely only on one or two of them to deal with the multitude of free radicals that we are exposed to. Some antioxidants need the protection and synergistic relationships that can only be provided by other antioxidants. Rather than taking an isolated extract of any one antioxidant, however "powerful", we should be ingesting a wide range of these vital compounds. The best way to ensure we do this is by eating a variety of antioxidant-rich foods.

☐ **The More, the Better?** Beyond a certain threshold, any beneficial substance can become harmful. Antioxidants are no exception, and yet they are often consumed in dangerously high quantities. Vitamin C, for example, is an essential vitamin and valuable antioxidant. Taken in large does, however, it has been found to damage DNA, *increasing* susceptibility to cancer. Even the antioxidants produced by our bodies can be damaging in excess. Bilirubin and uric acid are both beneficial antioxidants, but become dangerous if present in large quantities. Liver disease can, for example, lead to the very high levels of bilirubin that are responsible for the yellow skin discoloration known as jaundice. Kidney disease and gout are conditions associated with toxic levels of uric acid. The obvious solution is to eat moderate quantities of a wide variety of antioxidants. Again, the most effective way to do this is by eating a range of antioxidant-rich foods, such as spices.

Antioxidants: The Facts and the Fiction

☐ **All Thanks to Antioxidants?** Both scientists and the medical profession are often guilty of attributing the beneficial effects of certain foods exclusively to their constituent antioxidants and in so doing have often overlooked the multitude of other valuable phytochemicals these plants contain. Just as antioxidants work best in concert, so many other phytochemicals in foods contribute to their health-giving properties. No one type of compound can be expected to provide us with full protection, but by eating a range of foods rich in phytochemicals we can expect to receive optimal benefit from both antioxidants, as well as other bioactive substances. Examples of important non-antioxidant phytochemicals are black pepper's bioavailability enhancer, piperine, and the anticancer compounds zerumbone and sulphorane that are found in ginger and mustard respectively.

range of factors. These include psychological stress, infections, drugs, smoking, pollution, radiation, excessive exercise and obesity. Therefore we can all benefit from a regular intake of an array of antioxidants that can "mop up" excess free radicals as they are introduced into, and produced by, our bodies. Moreover, as many antioxidants are inactivated during the process of free radical neutralisation, they need to be continually replenished. Our bodies do some of the work by producing their own antioxidants, but we need to supplement these with food-based compounds.

▶ Strength in Diversity

The consumption of a wide array of antioxidants is essential if we are to provide ourselves with comprehensive protection against oxidative stress. As some of these are effective against certain free radicals but not others, consuming an assortment of antioxidants ensures that our bodies are able to tackle all types of free radical. This diversity also enables the antioxidants themselves to work optimally, as many operate synergistically with one another. Vitamin C, for instance, protects other antioxidants like vitamin E from being neutralised by free radicals. Moreover, different antioxidants tend to locate preferentially in different types of tissues and cells. For example, melatonin, an antioxidant hormone produced by the body, is a potent inhibitor of hydroxyl radicals. Unlike many antioxidants, it can cross the blood-brain barrier, and this property makes it particularly effective in protecting DNA in brain cells. The powerful antioxidants lycopene and vitamin E are only effective in lipid-containing areas, while yet other antioxidants work more efficiently in the "watery" areas of our tissues.

Although there is no doubt that food-derived antioxidants are an essential component for good health, there is still considerable debate as to which antioxidants are the most beneficial, and how much we require of each. These questions are unlikely to be answered soon or conclusively. Owing to the complex nature of the biological reactions involving antioxidants and free radicals, it is almost impossible to design studies that will give us the necessary information. What we can be sure of,

Strength in Diversity : The Mitochondrial Example

Mitochondria are cell structures that produce the energy required for all cellular processes. They are also the main producers of free radicals in our bodies – somewhat like our power stations or vehicle engines that release pollutants during the process of energy production. Between one and five percent of the oxygen used by mitochondria to generate energy results in the formation of superoxide radicals, which are particularly toxic and can damage both mitochondrial DNA and the mitochondrial membranes. Unlike the DNA in the cell nucleus, mitochondrial DNA has only a few DNA-repair enzymes and is thus very susceptible to superoxide free-radical damage. To complicate the situation, many antioxidants, including vitamins C and E, cannot get into the mitochondria to protect mitochondrial DNA from these free radicals. Certain food-derived antioxidants can, however, access the mitochondria to provide this protection. In this instance, as in many others, we obviously cannot rely only on one or two antioxidants as even very effective antioxidants like vitamins C and E have limited functions. Although they may be indispensable in dealing with some free-radical species, they are totally ineffective when it comes to neutralising others.

however, is that we do require outside sources of antioxidants to deal with the multiple sources of free-radical attack. Antioxidant-rich foods, in particular the spices, are an easy, effective and safe answer to the antioxidant dilemma.

▶ Bright and Tasty: Antioxidant-rich Foods

The best way to obtain a wide variety of antioxidants, in optimal amounts, is to eat an extensive selection of antioxidant-rich foods. As a general rule, strongly coloured or strongly flavoured plants contain the greatest quantity and range of antioxidant compounds.[2] Amongst the fruits, for example, the richly coloured berries, like blueberries, cranberries and raspberries, contain many antioxidants as do some other fruits, grains and vegetables. However, spices have one of the highest anti-oxidant concentrations of all food groups and are an ideal source of these vital compounds – some, like ginger, contain over 25 different anti-oxidants! Although all spices contain generous quantities of antioxidants, those richest in these substances are allspice, garlic, ginger, clove, cinnamon, lemon balm, oregano, peppermint, sage and thyme. By consuming these foods regularly we can do our bodies a tremendous service, providing them with a range of powerful weapons to fend off the daily onslaught by free radicals.

Spices Containing the Most Antioxidants

Allspice	Lemon balm
Black pepper	Oregano
Cinnamon	Peppermint
Clove	Sage
Ginger	Thyme

---

2 This rule also applies to other biologically active phytochemicals.

Cancer

CHAPTER 8

SUMMARY • SUMMARY • SUMMARY

- ☐ The fundamental cause of cancer is DNA damage that can occur as a result of aging, genetic susceptibility, and exposure to an assortment of carcinogens.
- ☐ Many of the phytochemicals found in spices act as potent preventive agents against cancer by defending DNA against free radicals and other toxins, preventing the overproduction of toxic chemicals within the body, assisting the body's detoxification processes and modulating a range of mechanisms involved in the development of cancer.
- ☐ In addition to reducing the risks of tumourigenesis, spices can also act as powerful treatments for some types of cancer.
- ☐ Some spices enhance the effects of the traditional cancer treatments of radiotherapy and chemotherapy, as well as reducing the negative side effects of these therapies.
- ☐ The most important anticancer spices are *anise, basil, black pepper, caraway, citrus, clove, fennel, garlic, ginger, green tea, mustard, rosemary, soy* and *turmeric*.

Cancer is a leading cause of death in most Western countries where, every year, hundreds of millions of dollars are allocated for research into new treatments. Eastern countries, where the incidence of most cancers is typically much lower, pour considerably less money into such investigations – and considerably more spices into their meals each year. These humble spices, it appears, are exceptionally good value for money. A growing body of epidemiological and clinical evidence suggests that the most important factor contributing to the difference in cancer incidence between the West and many Eastern countries can be attributed to the markedly higher levels of spice intake in the latter.

In the USA, for example, the three most lethal cancers are those of breast, prostate and lung. In India, the incidence of these same cancers – and of many others – is dramatically lower. Cancer of the breast occurs

75

eight times more frequently in American woman compared to their Indian counterparts; the incidence of prostate cancer in American men is more than 30 fold higher than in Indian men; and the incidence of lung cancer is almost 20 times higher in the USA than in India. Even taking into account lifestyle factors, the incidences of other diseases, and other demographic variables, these differences are remarkable. As scientists continue to study an increasing number of spices, new evidence confirms that many of these foods, both individually and in combination, do indeed have strong anticancer properties. By adding an average of 10 grams of spices a day to their meals, Indians, Sri Lankans, Thais and others are medicating themselves with some of the most powerful anticancer cocktails available.

There are a few effective modern cancer therapies that are used to treat and even cure some cancers. At the moment a number of promising drugs are in the development "pipelines" of pharmaceutical companies, some of which have been derived from spices. However, at least in the foreseeable future, treatments alone will not be enough to combat the disease that directly or indirectly touches all of us. Often invisible and asymptomatic for many months or even years, cancers are insidious and are frequently so far advanced by the time they are detected that attempts to treat them may be futile.

Reducing our susceptibility to cancer is one of the most important measures we can take to increase our chances of good health. This is not as difficult as it might sound. The following overview of the causes of cancer, the processes involved in its development and the multitude of ways in which phytochemicals act to combat it, shows that increasing our intake of spices is one of the most effective, convenient and economical ways in which we can fortify ourselves against this ubiquitous disease.

▶ Causes of Cancer

Cancer is caused by a range of factors, most of which follow directly from – or are exacerbated by – the aging process. As a result, the probability of getting cancer increases exponentially as we grow older.

The wide-ranging biochemical and chromosomal changes associated with aging increase the risk of DNA damage that is the first step towards developing a malignancy. If our biochemical processes fail to repair the DNA or destroy the cells in which it is contained the body's cancer-control mechanisms become ineffective and allow the unchecked proliferation of these abnormal, pre-malignant cells.

In addition to being less efficient at the repair and confinement of DNA damage, older bodies are less well equipped to protect cells against the agents that trigger the damage to our genetic coding material. Nevertheless, people of all ages can develop cancer, and youth is not guaranteed to protect against all carcinogenic factors. Among the most important of these are a genetic predisposition in the form of inherited oncogenes; exposure to environmental toxins, such as asbestos, petro-chemicals, tobacco, alcohol; viral infections, such as the herpes and wart viruses; radiation, including sunlight's ultraviolet rays; chronic inflammation, such as that arising from autoimmune disorders; and the production of excessive quantities of harmful endogenous chemicals, such as hydrogen pyroxide, by malfunctioning cellular processes.

These diverse carcinogens typically affect their damage via free radicals. Once produced within our body or introduced into our systems, highly reactive and destructive free-radical particles circulate in search of something to react with, or oxidize. Targets of this damaging oxidative process include DNA that, when attacked by free radicals, may cease to send the correct signals needed to prevent uncontrolled cell growth. It is for this reason that antioxidants, which react with and neutralise free radicals before they can attack our body, are such valuable substances to include in our diets. In addition to the many other anti-cancer properties found in spices, almost all of these foods contain powerful antioxidants which, when consumed regularly, mop up free radicals before they can initiate tumourigenesis.[1]

---

1 For further details about antioxidants refer to Chapter 7.

Spices are valuable preventive weapons against cancer not only for their antioxidant properties, but many of the phytochemicals contained in spices assist the body to detoxify and excrete carcinogenic compounds. Nor is the value of spices limited to their ability to prevent the first step of cancer development. Spices contain a number of powerful phytochemicals that act against pre-cancerous cells at each stage in their progression towards fully fledged tumours.

Table 3: Examples of the Anticancer Properties of Key Spices

All spices	Antioxidants
Cumin, pepper	Enhance antioxidant enzymes
Cumin, garlic, ginger, pepper	Inhibit cancer-associated inflammation
Ginger, pepper	Inhibit pro-inflammatory cytokines
Garlic, ginger, soy, turmeric	COX-2 inhibition
Citrus, ginger, pepper	Attack tumours directly
Anise, basil, capsicum, clove, cumin	Inhibit NF-κB
Fennel, garlic, ginger, rosemary, turmeric	Inhibit NF-κB
Citrus, garlic, grapes, green tea, mustard	Induce apoptosis
Brassicas, citrus, green tea, soy	Modulate autocrine loops and cell cycles
Green tea, turmeric, soy	Inhibit angiogenesis
Brassicas, caraway cumin	Neutralise carcinogenic toxins
Grapes, green tea, red wine	Reduce activated protein
Green tea, turmeric	Inhibit telomerase
Turmeric	Inhibit JAK-STAT pathway
Soy, turmeric	Inhibit oestrogen on hormone-dependent tumours
Green tea, soy, turmeric	Enhance chemotherapy and radiotherapy

The Properties of Cancer Cells

☐ Resistant to programmed cell death
☐ Cell division is rapid and uncontrolled
☐ Produce telomerase which renders cells immortal by stopping the loss of the telomeres at the end of chromosomes
☐ Produce their own growth factors in excessive amounts
☐ Insensitive to the body's growth inhibitors
☐ Secrete chemical signals that stimulate abnormal blood vessel growth
☐ Invade other tissue types and spread to distant sites in the body

▶ How Cancer Develops and Spreads

Cell division is a normal and essential physiological process that occurs in most tissues. In a normally functioning system there is a balance between cellular proliferation and programmed cell death (apoptosis) that is controlled by a complex but finely tuned biochemical web. Tumourigenesis is a multi-stage process, initiated when damage to the DNA of normal cells upsets the balance between apoptosis and cellular proliferation. This leads to further mutations and changes within the damaged cell, rapid proliferation of these abnormal cells, followed by invasion of adjacent tissues by the cancerous cells. Metastatic spread occurs when the cancer cells seed via the blood or lymphatic system to other organs.

Underlying this process is a more complex set of changes that occurs at cellular level. Nearly all cancers originate from a single cell, through the process of cell replication and division. However, a cell that degenerates into a tumour cell does not typically acquire all these properties at once, or in one generation. Instead, through a process known as *clonal evolution,* mutations are accumulated over time – division by division, and generation by generation. The more malignant the properties conveyed on a cell by a particular mutation, the greater an advantage it has over neighbouring cells, and the more likely it is to replicate and pass on its mutant genes. Eventually, as a result of this ruthless selection process, a tumour cell is formed. This process does not end with the acquisition of all the properties that characterise a tumour cell; later-stage, breakaway cancers are often more virulent than the early, primary tumours as even fully cancerous cells become stronger and more destructive over time.

This incremental development process has important implications for the prevention and treatment of cancers. Ideally, we should be preventing the onset of cancer by annihilating the early mutant cells before they can develop into fully fledged tumour cells. These pre-cancerous cells are, however, symptomless, making such an approach impractical if we were to try and use modern drugs. To take expensive drugs, with frequently risky and unpleasant side effects, in the hope of destroying early cancers that might not even exist, would clearly be unwise. In this respect, spices provide just what we are looking for. They contain compounds that are effective against pre-cancerous cells at different stages of their development, and by consuming spices regularly and in sufficient quantities, we provide the tools for our body to intercept tumours at the early stages of their development.

▶ Phytochemical Modulation of Underlying Cancer Processes

Over the last few decades, the phytochemicals contained in spices and in several other plants have been shown to modulate many of the mechanisms and processes involved in the development of cancer. Although we are just beginning to understand how they work, we know that many of these compounds counteract cancer either by enhancing the body's natural processes for combating tumourigenisis or by restoring the mechanisms that go awry as a result of cancerous mutations. Table 3 explains these mechanisms in greater detail.

Table 4: Key Mechanisms Involved in Cancer

Proto-oncogenes play a critical role in the control and release of chemical messengers that signal the cell to undergo cell division (mitosis), in order to produce more cells of a particular tissue. If these proto-oncogenes mutate, they become *oncogenes* that over-express the cell division signals responsible for the excessive cell division rates characteristic of cancer. A number of phytochemicals prevent the conversion of proto-oncogenes to the pathogenic oncogenes.

Tumour-suppressor Genes code for chemical messengers that slow or stop mitosis in order for DNA repair to occur. This is done via enzymes that detect DNA damage and prevent this fault being carried on to the next generation of cells. A mutation of the tumour-suppressor gene can result in its "switching off" capacity being compromised; this results in defective DNA being passed on to each succeeding generation of cells, where these defects become enhanced and eventually result in the development of tumour cells. The antioxidants in spices known to protect against cancer, notably those in *green tea, ginger, grapes* and *turmeric,* achieve this effect by preventing mutations in tumour-suppressor genes from occurring.

Nuclear Factor κ-B (NF-κB) is a protein involved in cell survival, cell adhesion, inflammation and cell growth, and is an essential cog in the biochemical machinery that controls the growth and proliferation of normal cells. However, its over-activation can be triggered by many of the carcinogens mentioned above, causing it to become an aggressive accelerator of tumourigenesis.[2] Extensive research in the last few years has shown that the pathway that activates this transcription factor can be interrupted by phytochemicals derived from spices including *anise, basil, capsicum, clove, cumin, fennel, garlic, ginger, rosemary* and *turmeric.*

Activated Protein (AP) is a molecule that, if produced in excess, stimulates the expression of several genes that enhance tumour proliferation, angiogenesis and tissue invasion. The effects of activated protein are blocked by phytochemicals in *green tea, turmeric* and *red wine.* These same compounds also interfere with the stimulatory effect of estrogens on certain hormone-dependent tumours.

---

2 The activation of NF-κB has also been linked to a variety of other diseases involving inflammation including atherosclerosis, myocardial infarction, diabetes, allergy, asthma, arthritis, Crohn's disease, multiple sclerosis, Alzheimer's disease, osteoporosis, psoriasis, septic shock, and AIDS.

Autocrine loops are part of cancer cell cycle feedback mechanisms whereby the tumour cells release chemical messengers (cytokines) that, in turn, stimulate further tumour proliferation. Cytokines do this by stimulating growth factor receptors on other cells, which produce more cytokines that further accelerate these positive-feedback autocrine loops. Several compounds, including those found in *mustard, citrus, green tea,* and *soy* either block the cell receptors or the action of the cancer cell cytokines themselves thus curtailing these self-sustaining processes.

The JAK-STAT pathway is a system of receptors, cytokines and enzymes that is part of an important stage common to the development of most tumour types. The *curcumin* found in *turmeric* in particular – along with other phytochemicals – has been found to have a strong inhibitory effect on this crucial tumourigenic mechanism.

Telomerase is an enzyme produced by cancer cells that stops the loss of telomeres from cancer cell DNA. Telomeres are the genes at the end of chromosomes that, in normal cells, are lost as each generation of cells duplicates itself. Telomerase interferes with this process and is one of the ways in which cancer cells achieve immortality. *Turmeric* and *green tea* amongst others contain phytochemicals that inhibit telomerase and so confer a finite lifespan on cancer cells.

Apoptosis (programmed cell death) is a built-in mechanism common to most normal cells. Cancer cells evade this inexorable process by means of several of the mechanisms outlined above. Phytochemicals isolated from several spices including, *citrus, garlic, green tea, mustard* and *grapes* have multiple functions that make them effective inhibitors of the processes that tumour cells have developed to evade apoptosis.

Angiogenesis is a normal process whereby the body produces blood vessels for new tissue growth and is activated by the secretion of various endogenous chemicals. Cancer cells also produce chemical signals that stimulate angiogenesis in the area where they are growing but this is usually an uncontrolled and haphazard process that produces abnormal blood vessels. Phytochemicals found in *green tea, turmeric* and *soy* inhibit angiogenesis of tumour cells thereby reducing the nourishment available to these cells and curtailing their invasion of adjacent tissues.

Cyclo-oxygenase-2 (COX-2) is an enzyme that, when overproduced, causes the chronic inflammation associated with many diseases such as arthritis. It is also over-expressed in almost all forms of cancer. Phytochemicals in *turmeric, garlic, ginger* and *soy* are all strong COX-2 inhibitors, and this property makes them indispensable foods in the fight to prevent and treat not only cancer but a wide range of other conditions where COX-2 enzymes are causative factors.

Radiotherapy and chemotherapy are widely used but imperfect treatments for cancer. Not only do they have serious, debilitating side effects, but tumour cells often develop resistance to these therapeutic modalities. Moreover, in addition to their intended destruction of cancerous cells, these therapies frequently activate NF-κB, thereby contributing to the suppression of apoptosis and the promotion of tumour proliferation – just the opposite of what one would like from a cancer treatment. Chemotherapy and radiotherapy also activate COX-2 enzymes, thus aggravating the inflammatory process that underlies many cancers. Several phytochemicals, found in high quantities in *turmeric, soy* and *green tea*, reduce the activation of COX-2 and sensitize the tumour cells to both radiotherapy and chemotherapy, enhancing their therapeutic effect.

| CHAPTER | 9 | Cardiovascular Disease |

S U M M A R Y • S U M M A R Y • S U M M A R Y

☐ Atherosclerosis, the underlying cause of cardiovascular disease, is characterised by the deposition of cholesterol plaques in the lining of the arteries that may rupture and result in a heart attack or stroke.

☐ Cardiovascular disease is associated with a range of factors including raised cholesterol and triglyceride levels, high blood pressure, sticky platelets, obesity, smoking, diabetes and chronic systemic inflammation.

☐ Spices are powerful preventative agents against cardiovascular disease, as they modify most risk factors as well as other illnesses and pathological processes associated with this condition.

☐ *Caper, cinnamon, citrus, coriander, fenugreek, garlic, ginger, grapes, mustard, oregano, rosemary, soy, thyme* are examples of spices that exhibit powerful, protective effects against the development of heart attacks and strokes.

☐ Although the term **cardiovascular disease** includes any disease that affects the heart and blood vessels, it is commonly used to refer to those diseases caused by atherosclerosis.

☐ **Atherosclerosis** is a pathological process characterized by the deposition of cholesterol- and calcium-containing **atheromatous plaques** in the lining of the coronary, cerebral and other arteries. In their earlier stages of development atheromatous deposits do not cause narrowing of the arteries but inhibit their ability to dilate; in this way they restrict the flow of blood during times of increased oxygen demand by heart muscle and other tissues.

84

The most important cardiovascular diseases are heart attack and stroke, which are responsible for more deaths in the West than any other illness.[1] They kill approximately one million Americans and over four million Europeans each year and account for over 50 percent of deaths in these regions. In the USA alone, over 50 million people suffer from cardio-vascular-related problems.

As the principal scourge of the West – and increasingly of developing countries that adopt Western lifestyle habits – vast sums of money are devoted to combating cardiovascular disease. Success is made more elusive as a result of the multitude of risk and causative factors contributing to its underlying pathology including, amongst others, high cholesterol, high blood pressure, smoking and obesity. Efforts to counteract cardiovascular disease are currently aimed at several levels: from public health programmes that aim to improve dietary habits, reduce obesity and curtail smoking, to the provision of drugs that ameliorate the major risk factors and underlying conditions such hypertension, atherosclerosis and "sticky" platelets. Some of the most successful medicines used in this context are aspirin and drugs like clopidogrel that reduce platelet aggregation (stickiness) and prevent abnormal blood clotting, statins that lower high blood lipid levels, and antihypertensive drugs. While these medicines can be extremely effective, each only counteracts this multifaceted disease in one or two ways, and by the time they are prescribed irreversible damage may already have occurred.

Given its devastating consequences for so many of us, we all need to pre-empt and fight cardiovascular disease as early on in its development as possible. In addition to other lifestyle modifications, spices provide an ideal means to do this; they enable us to slow or halt the progression of

---

1 While this book refers principally to the two biggest cardiovascular killers, heart disease and thrombotic stroke, there are other forms of cardiovascular disease including peripheral vascular disease and haemorrhagic stroke. Many of the spices mentioned in this chapter also protect against these diseases.

the disease before we reach the stage at which prescription drugs become necessary. Not only do the phytochemicals in many spices act by lowering cholesterol and preventing abnormal blood clotting, they also counteract a range of processes involved in the development of cardiovascular disease and simultaneously protect against other illnesses too. This chapter outlines the major risk factors and pathological processes involved in the development of cardiovascular disease and describes the variety of ways in which spices can prevent or slow the progression of this condition.

▶ Risk Factors for Cardiovascular Disease

Cardiovascular disease is associated with a wide range of lifestyle and other risk factors. The most important of these are elevated cholesterol and triglyceride levels, high blood pressure, sticky platelets, smoking, obesity, raised homocysteine levels, genetic predisposition, and related illnesses such as diabetes. To complicate matters, many of these factors are inter-linked and exacerbate one other. Smoking, for instance, also raises blood pressure; obesity increases the chances of developing diabetes and high blood lipid levels, both of which are also associated with a genetic pre-disposition to these conditions. Aging on its own and, more so, when associated with weight gain and reduced exercise, is also a major risk factor.

▶ Cholesterol and Other Lipids

High blood lipid levels are among the most important of the risk factors associated with cardiovascular disease. Normally cholesterol plays a central role in the production of several crucial hormones and is an important component of cell walls. Similarly triglycerides are not dangerous as long as their blood levels remain normal, and it is only in excess that these lipids become threats to our health. Raised levels of cholesterol and triglycerides, as well as imbalances in their lipoprotein carrier proteins, have all been directly implicated as major risk factors underlying cardiovascular disease. These lipid imbalances can, in turn, be

Major Risk Factors for Cardiovascular Disease

- ☐ Raised blood lipid (cholesterol and triglyceride) levels
- ☐ High blood pressure
- ☐ Sticky platelets
- ☐ Obesity
- ☐ Smoking
- ☐ High homocysteine levels
- ☐ Diabetes
- ☐ Chronic systemic inflammation
- ☐ Oral contraception and hormone replacement therapy
- ☐ Lack of exercise
- ☐ Age

caused by a number of factors, including genetic predisposition, high dietary fat intake and liver disease.

Of the blood lipids, cholesterol – a major constituent of atheromatous plaques – is the one most closely linked to cardiovascular disease. Blood levels of cholesterol may become abnormally high for a number of reasons. Usually the imbalance can be attributed to either a genetic predisposition or a diet high in saturated fats commonly found in animal products. Once ingested, dietary cholesterol is broken down in the intestines and then re-synthesized in the liver before being released into the blood stream. Although the cholesterol in our blood is not exactly the same as that found in the food that we eat, an excessive dietary intake may increase the risk of high blood cholesterol levels. Irrespective of whether diet or genes are ultimately responsible, high levels of cholesterol and other lipids dramatically increase the risk of cardiovascular disease. Blood lipid imbalances contribute directly to the development of atherosclerosis which, in turn, can lead to a heart attack or stroke.

▶ Atheromatous Plaque Formation

The deposition of cholesterol and triglycerides in the arteries is the fundamental process underlying the development of atherosclerosis. As these lipids are insoluble in water, they need to be transported in the blood by water-soluble lipoprotein carrier molecules. The most important of these "molecular suitcases" are low density lipoprotein (LDL) and high density lipoprotein (HDL) which shuttle cholesterol and triglyceride back and forth between the liver and other tissues. HDL and LDL are both cholesterol transporters, but they have different functions. LDL carries cholesterol *to* the tissues, and arteries whereas HDL carries it back *from* these areas to be processed by the liver and excreted in the bile.

Once delivered to the artery by its LDL carrier, cholesterol is oxidised. This oxidative process precipitates an inappropriate immune response, and the ensuing inflammation causes damage to the blood vessels resulting in the deposition of calcium, cholesterol and other substances in the endothelial lining of the arteries. Eventually, sufficient quantities of these substances accumulate to form an atheromatous plaque. The process is accelerated if there is insufficient HDL to remove the cholesterol from the tissues and take it back to the liver. This is the reason that *high* LDL, cholesterol and triglyceride levels and *low* HDL levels are associated with *increased* risk of heart disease, and why we need to keep LDL levels low and HDL levels high.

Atheromatous plaque formation is associated with an inflammatory process involving the oxidation of LDL cholesterol. The mechanism underlying this process is currently under intensive investigation and is thought to be associated with a low grade pathological state called chronic systemic inflammation. Spices like garlic, ginger, oregano, rosemary, thyme and

Examples of Drugs and Spices with Similar Functions

Effect	Prescription Drugs	Spice Equivalents
Lower blood lipids	Statins	*Cinnamon, citrus, coriander, fenugreek, garlic, ginger, grapes, oregano, rosemary, soy, star anise, thyme*
Lower blood pressure	Beta blockers ACE inhibitors Calcium channel blockers Diuretics	*Garlic, grapes, green tea*
Reduce platelet stickiness	Aspirin Clopidogrel	*Cloves, garlic, ginger, onion, oregano, rosemary, thyme*

others contain anti-inflammatory phytochemicals that inhibit this abnormal inflammatory condition. Antioxidants present in most spices also play a major role in preventing the oxidation of LDL cholesterol.

▶ Atherosclerosis

The principal cause of heart attack and thrombotic stroke is athero-sclerosis-related pathology. If an atheromatous plaque ruptures into a coronary or cerebral artery, it may block the blood flow to parts of the heart or brain, respectively. The oxygen starvation associated with the reduced blood flow is responsible for the often lethal damage that occurs during these events.

Although the precise mechanisms associated with the development of atherosclerosis have not been fully elucidated, some of these processes, and their associated risk factors, are well understood. Its formation typically begins during the teenage years, but the process may be accelerated by poor lifestyle habits. In Western countries today it is not unusual for atherosclerosis to start in young children, resulting in these unfortunate individuals developing the symptoms of cardiovascular disease in early adulthood. Consisting mainly of calcified, cholesterol compounds, atheromatous plaques cause a gradual narrowing and hardening of the arteries. This restricts blood flow to tissues, and places extra strain on the heart which has to work harder to pump blood through stiff, narrow blood vessels. Once the plaques occlude more than 50 percent of the lumen of the arteries, cardiovascular disease begins to manifest itself in the form of angina, heart attack and stroke.

▶ "Sticky" Platelets

The risk of a heart attack or stroke resulting from atherosclerosis is increased in the presence of sticky platelets. Platelets are small cells found in the blood that are involved in the inflammatory response. They are also crucial components of blood clots that help to control bleeding by sticking to one another and, in so doing, help to contain bleeding from damaged

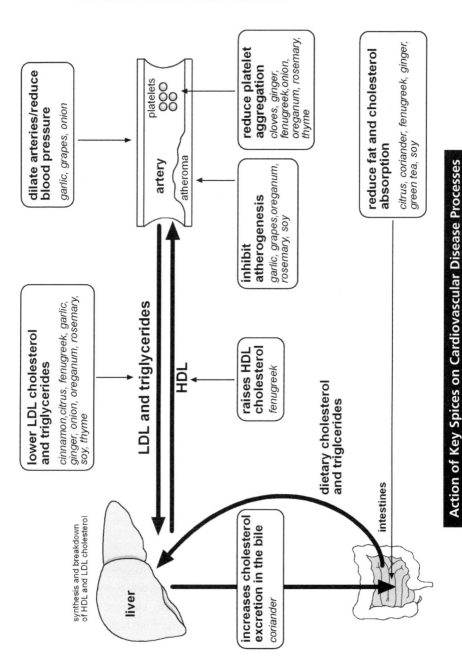

dilate arteries/reduce blood pressure
garlic, grapes, onion

platelets

artery

atheroma

reduce platelet aggregation
cloves, ginger, fenugreek, onion, oreganum, rosemary, thyme

inhibit atherogenesis
garlic, grapes, oreganum, rosemary, soy

reduce fat and cholesterol absorption
citrus, coriander, fenugreek, ginger, green tea, soy

lower LDL cholesterol and triglycerides
cinnamon, citrus, fenugreek, garlic, ginger, onion, oreganum, rosemary, soy, thyme

LDL and triglycerides

HDL

raises HDL cholesterol
fenugreek

dietary cholesterol and triglcerides

synthesis and breakdown of HDL and LDL cholesterol

liver

increases cholesterol excretion in the bile
coriander

intestines

Action of Key Spices on Cardiovascular Disease Processes

blood vessels. Platelets can, however, become a health liability if they are too "sticky" and adhere to one another even when there is no bleeding. If this abnormal aggregation involves a significant number of platelets, a clot may develop. Clot formation may also be precipitated by the rupture of an atheromatous plaque into the lumen of a blood vessel. The more "sticky" the platelets are, the more likely they are to aggregate on the ruptured plaque.

▶ Heart Attack and Thrombotic Stroke

Over time, cholesterol and calcium continue to be deposited in the artery walls, causing the blood vessels to narrow thereby reducing the flow of blood to the tissues. As they grow in size, the atheromatous plaques become unstable and may rupture into the lumen of an artery, causing permanent blockage to the blood supply. Plaque rupture stimulates platelet aggregation and clot formation at the site of the plaque, and this causes further narrowing of the vessel and aggravation of the already impeded blood flow. This process occurring in a coronary artery is the fundamental cause of a heart attack. The same event taking place in a cerebral artery may cause a thrombotic stroke, either by blocking an artery at the point of rupture, or by causing a blockage elsewhere in the brain after a piece of the clot becomes dislodged and travels to a smaller, more distant, blood vessel.

Cardioprotective Properties of Some Key Spices	
Blood pressure control	*Garlic, grapes, green tea*
Lower LDL cholesterol	*Caper, coriander, cinnamon, citrus, fenugreek, garlic, grape, ginger, soy*
LDL antioxidant	*Ginger, oregano, rosemary, star anise, thyme*
Reduce platelet aggregation	*Clove, ginger, onion, oregano, rosemary, thyme*
Lower homocysteine levels	*Mustard and other brassicas*
Anti-inflammatory	*Bay leaf, garlic, ginger, oregano,rosemary, thyme, turmeric*

❱ The "Polypill" Concept

Given the multitude of risk factors and pathological mechanisms involved in the development of heart disease and stroke, it makes sense to adopt a multifaceted approach to prevention. In this respect those with cardio-vascular disease are currently prescribed drugs to treat the risk factors appropriate to their condition. However, some experts have gone one step further and proposed that *all* those over a certain age, regardless of their health status, should take a daily "polypill". This would contain statin drugs to lower blood lipid levels, aspirin to reduce platelet aggregation, and other drugs that lower blood pressure and homocysteine levels.

The proponents of the polypill concept claim that overall it could reduce cardiovascular mortality by more than 80 percent. However, this shotgun approach has yet to be embraced by the medical profession as a whole. The main reason is that almost all of the drugs it would contain have potential side effects. Statins, for instance, can have pro-inflammatory effects, exacerbating what is already an inflammatory process. Aspirin can cause intestinal bleeding, and drugs to lower blood pressure can result in arrhythmias (irregular heart beats) and other adverse effects.

Fortunately, we do not need to wait for a risky polypill to become available. Spices contain phytochemicals which have similar beneficial effects to all the components of the proposed polypill. *Cinnamon* and *fenugreek* reduce blood lipids and lower LDL levels. *Ginger* reduces platelet aggregation, *garlic* and *green tea* lower blood pressure, and *brassica plants*, such as mustard, lower homocysteine levels. Spices also have additional benefits, offering their own effective shotgun approach to the prevention of cardiovascular disease. The wide range of phyto-chemicals contained in spices is capable of modifying all the processes implicated in the development of the disease. Spices also combat diseases such as diabetes, obesity and other conditions associated with cardio-vascular disease. By giving ourselves a daily dose of these powerful, protective spices, we are counteracting a multitude of pathological processes that collectively pose a greater risk to our health than any other medical condition.

Diabetes

CHAPTER 10

S U M M A R Y • S U M M A R Y • S U M M A R Y

- ☐ Type I and Type II diabetes and metabolic syndrome are related diseases that are all associated with abnormal glucose metabolism.
- ☐ Obesity is implicated as a cause of both metabolic syndrome and Type II diabetes.
- ☐ The phytochemicals found in a variety of spices help to control many of the pathological mechanisms that underlie diabetes and metabolic syndrome.
- ☐ *Cinnamon, fenugreek, garlic, coriander, ginger* and *caper* are the spices most effective in lowering blood glucose and abnormal blood lipids in these diseases.

Diabetes is one of the top five most significant diseases in the developed world and is rapidly becoming a heavy burden in the developing world as well. Today more than 150 million people worldwide suffer from diabetes, and this staggering figure is expected to double by 2025. Type I diabetes accounts for a relatively small proportion of diabetes cases whereas Type II diabetes, which is closely associated with overweight and obesity, is the predominant of the two disease subtypes.

Both forms of the disease affect the body's ability to metabolise glucose, which can have severely damaging and sometimes lethal consequences. The processes underlying the development of diabetes relate primarily to the production of, or sensitivity to, insulin, which is the principal hormone responsible for controlling the body's utilization of glucose. Treatment of diabetes involves dietary management, exercise and the use of oral hypoglycaemic drugs or insulin injections.

Spices can be remarkably effective against diabetes, both by preventing and controlling established disease. The phytochemicals contained in some spices are capable of directly counteracting the underlying disease mechanisms; by stimulating insulin production, raising insulin sensitivity and modulating the absorption of glucose in the intestines. Spices can also combat associated conditions such as obesity, in addition to other pathological mechanisms implicated in this disease.

The Role of Insulin

Insulin is a hormone produced by the islet cells of the pancreas. These cells secrete insulin into the bloodstream in response to the rise of blood glucose that occurs following the ingestion of carbohydrates. Insulin then binds to receptors on the surface of cells causing them to absorb glucose from the blood stream. It also controls the conversion of glucose into energy stores in the form of glycogen in muscle and liver cells, and fat in adipose tissue. When blood glucose levels decrease, insulin production falls to a certain point where it remains until further carbohydrates are ingested and absorbed from the intestines. This mechanism is finely tuned and, in healthy people, keeps blood glucose levels within a narrow range. If there is insufficient, or no response, to insulin the cells are effectively starved of glucose, and blood glucose levels become dangerously elevated. Insulin works in concert with several other hormones, therefore abnormalities in both its production and performance can have a wide range of adverse consequences.

❱ Sub-types of Diabetes and Metabolic Syndrome

Type I Diabetes (juvenile onset diabetes), usually starts in childhood or early adulthood and accounts for less than 10 percent of the total number of diabetics. The exact cause of this sub-type is unclear but it is believed to be an autoimmune disease, which is precipitated by some environmental "trigger", such as a virus. This leads to an inappropriate immune response involving the destruction of the insulin-producing cells of the pancreas. Individuals who develop this disease can no longer adequately metabolise blood glucose and must have daily insulin injections for the remainder of their lives. The insulin regime has to be strictly controlled, as too much insulin can result in hypoglycaemia (very low blood sugar) and potentially death. Conversely, failure to provide supplemental insulin will lead to hyperglycaemia (very high blood sugar), coma and death. In between these two dangerous extremes is a zone where the patient is not at immediate risk of dying. However, even within the non-lethal range of blood glucose concentrations, inadequate treatment may lead to severe complications such as cardiovascular disease, kidney failure, circulatory impairment, nerve damage, cataracts and infections.

Type II Diabetes (maturity onset diabetes) was, as its old name suggests, associated with people of middle age or older. But with dietary changes – notably the increased consumption of processed, fatty and sugary foods – and the incidence of obesity relentlessly increasing, it is not uncommon for people in their teens to develop the disease. Unlike Type I diabetes, where there is insufficient insulin production, in Type II diabetes the pancreas produces normal or greater than normal quantities of insulin. However, the biochemical abnormalities that arise in the latter type manifest themselves as *insulin resistance.* These defects cause hyperglycaemia by interfering with the normal function of insulin and thereby glucose uptake into the cells. The increased levels of fat oxidation commonly found in Type II diabetics are also considered to be a cause of insulin resistance.

Metabolic Syndrome, which is also known as Syndrome X or Insulin Resistance Syndrome is not only considered a disease in its own right, but is also a precursor to Type II diabetes and increases the risk of cardiovascular disease and stroke. Metabolic Syndrome is characterized by insulin resistance, high blood pressure, elevated triglyceride levels, low HDL levels and central obesity (fat accumulation around the abdomen and abdominal organs). To compensate for the unresponsiveness to insulin, the pancreas produces more insulin. This destabilises several metabolic processes, leading to tissue and organ damage.

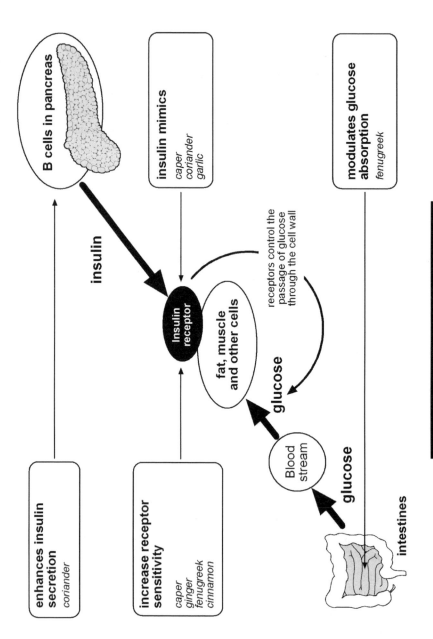

Antidiabetic Properties of Key Spices

B cells in pancreas

insulin mimics
caper
coriander
garlic

modulates glucose absorption
fenugreek

insulin

Insulin receptor

fat, muscle and other cells

receptors control the passage of glucose through the cell wall

glucose

enhances insulin secretion
coriander

increase receptor sensitivity
caper
ginger
fenugreek
cinnamon

Blood stream

glucose

glucose

intestines

96

◗ Insulin Resistance

In order to understand the approaches to the prevention and control of metabolic syndrome and Type II diabetes, it is helpful to consider the processes underlying insulin resistance. Before a cell will allow glucose through its protective membrane, its insulin receptor must be "turned on" by insulin or a chemical mimic. Insulin resistance occurs when the receptor develops a weakened response to insulin resulting in the cell's failure to absorb sufficient quantities of glucose from the blood. This results in energy deprivation for the cells and raised blood glucose levels. The primary cause of this weakened insulin receptor response is the chronic over-production of insulin. Not only does *too much* insulin lead to receptor failure, but wide *fluctuations* in insulin levels are also known to be an important cause of this condition. These oscillating levels are, in turn, closely associated with a diet high in refined carbohydrate foods.

◗ Diet and Insulin Receptor Failure

Extreme changes of insulin levels are typically the result of a diet dominated by a high intake of refined carbohydrate foods. Products such as sugar, sweetened soft drinks and white bread, are absorbed quickly from the intestines into the blood stream causing a sudden rise in blood glucose levels. These foods are said to have a "high glycemic index", or high GI, because of their rapid absorption and the resulting peak in blood glucose levels. In order to stimulate the cells to absorb this sudden glucose load, the pancreas responds by releasing larger than normal quantities of insulin. The excessive amount of insulin produced to achieve this effect results in a sudden fall in blood glucose, and within a couple of hours this level becomes very low. The subsequent intake of more high GI foods causes the blood glucose to rise dramatically once more, perpetuating the cycle of wildly fluctuating glucose and insulin levels. If this steady bombardment of the receptors by large amounts of insulin continues over a long period, it eventually causes their malfunction and insensitivity. It is a bit like repeatedly forcing an oversized key into a lock. After a while, the excessive wear and tear caused by the large key results in damage to the lock making it increasingly harder to turn. If this continues for long enough, the lock wears out and fails to work altogether.

Glycemic Index (GI)

The glycemic index categorises carbohydrates according to how rapidly they cause blood glucose levels to rise.

High GI foods, which should generally be eaten sparingly, cause a rapid rise in blood glucose. These include refined carbohydrates such as sugar, sweets, sweetened cold drinks, white bread, some fruits and certain starchy vegetables such as potatoes.

Low GI foods are slowly absorbed and allow blood glucose to rise gradually. These foods include unrefined carbohydrates, such as whole grains, as well as most legumes and vegetables.

The protein and fat components of foods may change the GI of individual carbohydrates.

▶ Less Sugar, More Spice

A good diet is one of the most effective ways to prevent insulin resistance. The consumption of predominantly *low* GI foods means that insulin is released slowly. As a result, glucose is absorbed by cells in a controlled manner and blood glucose levels do not rise and fall so rapidly. This prevents the harmful glucose – and thus insulin – peaks and troughs that are associated with the repeated ingestion of large quantities of high GI foods. Reducing the proportion of high GI foods in the diet has another, indirect benefit in terms of preventing insulin resistance. Such foods are typically fattening and reducing their intake can lead to weight loss.

Obesity, and particularly central obesity, is another important cause of insulin resistance and tackling it is an effective way to reduce the risk of diabetes and other chronic diseases.

Another invaluable dietary tool for preventing and managing insulin resistance and diabetes are the spices. These foods counter the disease processes in several ways and can be tremendously helpful, irrespective of whether individuals are making dietary or other lifestyle changes. Moreover, because of the range of ways in which spices act against this disease, they can be useful in both Type I and Type II diabetes and in metabolic syndrome.

Cinnamon, for example, is a potent inducer of insulin sensitivity and the addition of as little as one gram a day to the diet can reduce the blood glucose levels of diabetics by a staggering 30 percent. It does this by enhancing the enzymes that increase insulin receptor sensitivity and inhibiting those enzymes with the opposite action. Cinnamon has the added benefit of lowering the abnormal lipid levels commonly found in diabetics and reducing the oxidative stress caused by lipid oxidation in these patients. *Fenugreek* is also highly effective at modulating glucose metabolism and can lower the blood glucose levels of diabetics by up to 45 percent. This spice both increases insulin receptor sensitivity and normalizes the imbalanced blood lipid levels of diabetics. The fibre

Safety Note

The spices mentioned in this chapter are powerful agents against diabetes. In some cases they can control diabetes on their own; in others, they are valuable adjuncts to the orthodox treatment and management of the disease. All diabetics should, however, notify their doctors before taking larger than normal quantities of these spices. They should also continue to monitor their blood sugar levels. Spices known to help diabetics do not adversely affect the blood glucose levels of non-diabetics, but when consumed regularly by these individuals they can help to prevent the onset of diabetes and metabolic syndrome.

contained in fenugreek also lowers the GI of a meal, thus modulating the post-prandial blood glucose levels by slowing the absorption of high GI foods. Several other spices also have valuable properties. *Ginger* and *caper* increase sensitivity to insulin, and caper mimics the effects of insulin. *Garlic* and *coriander* are also insulin mimics, while coriander enhances insulin secretion. Most spices can, with their rich array of antioxidants, help to prevent the complications of diabetes by reducing the oxidation of fats.

A small number of simple spices possess an amazing potency and range of weapons in the fight against diabetes. By helping to prevent, delay and even treat one of the worst and most widespread chronic diseases afflicting the modern world, they offer some of today's most remarkable dietary drugs.

Anti diabetic Effects of Key Spices

Increase insulin sensitivity	*Capers, cinnamon, fenugreek, ginger*
Mimic effects of insulin	*Capers, coriander, garlic*
Enhances insulin secretion	*Coriander*
Modulates glucose absorption	*Fenugreek*
Lower blood lipids	*Cinnamon, fenugreek*
Reduces oxidative stress from fat oxidation	*Cinnamon*

Alzheimer's Disease

Alzheimer's Disease

CHAPTER 11

S U M M A R Y • S U M M A R Y • S U M M A R Y

☐ Alzheimer's disease is an age-related degenerative condition of the brain that leads to dementia and possibly death.
☐ It occurs in up to 50 percent of 85 year olds in the West. In India the extremely low incidence of AD has been linked to high levels of *turmeric* consumption.
☐ The precise cause of AD is unknown but several factors are known to be associated with its development.
☐ *Turmeric, rosemary, ginger* and *garlic* show impressive protective and curative effects against this disease.

Alzheimer's disease (AD) is a debilitating and ultimately lethal neuro-degenerative disorder that currently afflicts about 18 million people worldwide. The incidence of the disease increases exponentially with age and, with life expectancy increasing in many parts of the world, global prevalence is expected to double by 2025. Alzheimer's disease is characterised by progressive intellectual deterioration, starting with memory loss that is followed by intellectual impairment, poor decision making, uncoordinated movements, speech impediments and loss of recognition of familiar people and places. The causes of AD are poorly understood and effective preventative or therapeutic drugs have yet to be developed.

In most Western nations, AD is the commonest cause of dementia and one of the most devastating and prevalent diseases amongst the elderly. In these countries more than 2 percent of people over the age of 65 show signs of the disease while up to 50 percent of 80 year olds show symptoms of AD. Although the incidence of AD is increasing rapidly in many developing countries, on the Indian subcontinent it remains extremely rare, even among the high-risk age groups. Recent studies have associated this reduced risk primarily with the consumption of turmeric that, together with several other spices, has been shown to have protective and curative effects against the disease.

Spices Known To Help Prevent Alzheimer's Disease			
☐ Turmeric	☐ Rosemary	☐ Garlic	☐ Ginger

▶ Causes of Alzheimer's Disease

The causes of AD are not fully understood, but there are several pathological processes that occur in those afflicted with the disease. The most prominent of these is the deposition of an abnormal protein, amyloid, in the brains of Alzheimer's disease sufferers. Amyloid is deposited in the form of plaques between the neurons and also accumulates in the walls of small blood vessels in the brain, where it impedes the flow of blood to brain tissues. The aggregation inside the neurones of abnormal amounts of *tau* protein filaments is another pathological feature of AD. A further process associated with the disease is atrophy, or wasting, of nerve tissue which leads to the loss of synapses and their associated neurotransmitter chemicals from key areas of the brain. In all cases, the precise causes of these pathological processes are unclear but they and certain other factors appear to increase the risk and aggravate the development of AD.

Some Factors Associated with Alzheimer's Disease
☐ Exposure to excessive amounts of potentially toxic metals like *aluminium, copper* and *zinc* has been associated with AD.
☐ Chronic *oxidative stress* is being investigated as one of the pathological processes underlying the development of the disease.
☐ *Chronic systemic inflammation* may also be a causative factor, as recent studies have found that individuals who take aspirin and other non-steroidal anti-inflammatory drugs on a regular basis have much lower incidences of AD than those who do not take these drugs.
☐ There is evidence that genetic factors may play a minor role as a cause of AD.

▶ Spices and the Prevention of Alzheimer's Disease

As pharmaceutical companies battle – as yet unsuccessfully – to find either preventive or curative drugs for Alzheimer's disease, potent weapons against it already exist in the form of several common spices.

Confirming epidemiological pointers that diet plays a key role in AD's low incidence in India are several promising laboratory studies of the phytochemical *curcumin*. Found in large quantities in turmeric, curcumin has been shown to inhibit the deposition of amyloid in the brain and, in some cases, actually reverse this process. Studies have also shown that *rosmarinic acid*, present in rosemary and several other spices as well as *gingerol* and *zingerone* found in ginger (which also contains curcumin) have similar protective effects. Although these are the most thoroughly researched spices in respect of AD, evidence is accumulating that several others, including *garlic*, have similar preventive effects against this disorder. Moreover, it is almost certain that the list of spices shown to protect us against AD will continue to grow. In particular, the preventive effect of long-term ingestion of aspirin suggests that the many salicylate-rich spices confer similar protection against this illness.

Research continues to reveal that, as in the case of other degenerative diseases, there are multiple underlying processes responsible for AD, toxic metal accumulation, oxidative stress and chronic systemic inflammation being the prime suspects. Once again it seems obvious that to prevent the disease from occurring, we should take a shotgun approach; by using spices and other foods that provide an array of chemical compounds we will protect ourselves against the processes that are known to underlie this condition. In all likelihood the wide range of actions exhibited by the chemicals in spices also counteract other, yet undiscovered, processes or toxins associated with AD.

Alzheimer's disease could affect any one of us and, as spices are the only known defence we have against this debilitating illness, these remarkable foods are medicines we cannot afford to go without.

CHAPTER 12

Aging

S U M M A R Y • S U M M A R Y • S U M M A R Y

☐ Aging is a complex, multifaceted process that is influenced by both genetic and environmental factors.

☐ The processes underlying aging are common to many age-related illnesses. The risk of cancer, heart disease and other chronic diseases increases as we move through middle age and beyond.

☐ As it ages the body becomes less effective at defending itself against environmental stresses like poor diet, tobacco smoke and other toxins that, in turn, accelerate the aging process as well as increasing the risk of disease.

☐ Aging can be retarded by the same antioxidants and other phyto-chemicals that help prevent the onset of degenerative diseases.

Aging, or senescence, is an inevitable, ultimately destructive process that affects all of us. However, its underlying mechanisms are multi-faceted and various tissue and cell types tend to start aging at different stages during our lives. There are a number of ways in which we can interfere with these factors and thereby retard the overall process of aging. In so doing, not only do we assist our bodies to continue to function for longer, but we increase our chances of good health well into old age by protecting ourselves against debilitating and often deadly chronic diseases.

There is a very close relationship between aging and degenerative diseases: the processes underlying aging inflict damage that increases susceptibility to disease; and many of the pathological agents and processes that are the direct causes of degenerative diseases also expedite, and are integral to, the aging process. An appreciation of this two-way relationship and of the numerous, inextricable links between aging and degenerative diseases is critical to understand how to prolong life and sustain good health. The aging-disease relationship is particularly relevant to the role of spice-derived phytochemicals as many of the mechanisms through which these substances exert disease-preventing properties can also help to slow aging.

▶ How and Why We Age

Aging involves numerous, complex processes but it ultimately manifests itself in several broad ways: a declining ability to respond appropriately to all types of stresses, homeostatic imbalances, an increased risk of disease and eventually death. The effects of aging become most evident in the deteriorating appearance and function of tissues and organs that ultimately affects the whole organism. However, the less obvious biochemical processes of aging occur at cellular level. The cellular processes underlie the visible effects of aging and while their causes are not fully understood, we know that some are programmed into our genes; others – in the form of DNA mutations, toxin damage, and the general stresses of life – are the "un-programmed" consequences of wear and tear and the sundry destructive processes that occur over time.

▶ Genetically Programmed Processes

A key way in which our genes effect and coordinate cellular aging is thought to involve the segments of DNA at the end of chromosomes called *telomeres*. The majority of cells in our body replicate through mitosis, with each division producing a near exact copy of the parent cell. This process enables our body to grow, and to replenish damaged or diseased cells. With time, however, the rate of division slows and, eventually, many cells stop replicating altogether. Telomeres are believed to underlie this *replicative senescence,* as with each division they shorten, thereby imposing a limit to the number of divisions that can occur. In addition to a finite replicative capacity, our cells have a finite lifespan, exhibiting *cellular senescence.* As lost cells are no longer replaced by mitosis, total cell numbers in certain key tissues, including the heart, may decrease with time.

Given our body's numerous repair and defence mechanisms, it is not unreasonable to ask why our cells are ultimately designed to die. Senescence is certainly not an inevitable feature of cellular life: it is not, for example, observed in single-celled organisms that reproduce through mitotic cell division; nor does cellular senescence exist in many other simple organisms, such as sponges, corals and even lobsters whose cells are said to be *biologically immortal*. The reason for the cellular senescence exhibited by complex organisms is not fully understood but is thought, at least in part, to be a built-in control against cancer which relies on uncontrolled cell proliferation and cell immortality.

▶ Degenerative Processes

In addition to its programmed facets – in the form of cellular and replicative senescence – aging involves general damage and wear on our cells, tissues and organs. Caused by DNA mutations, toxins and other destructive agents, these degenerative processes, that include oxidation and inflammation, are in many cases common to both aging and chronic diseases.

DNA mutations that induce cell immortality are, for example, integral to the development of cancer. And while mutations may occur at any time, the likelihood that they will overcome the immune system and cause disease increases exponentially as we enter middle age and beyond. This is owing to the fact that when cells divide by mitosis, they replicate their entire complement of chromosomal DNA and mutations that occur before or during replication are passed on to the next generation of DNA. While a single mutation may not cause cancer or other diseases, over time and many generations, mutations accumulate thereby increasing the probability that they will trigger cancerous and other pathological processes. The number of divisions a cell has gone through is one risk factor for disease-inducing mutations in DNA; another is the exposure to external or internally produced toxins that can damage many other cellular structures in addition to DNA.

The impact and risk posed by toxins and other damaging environmental stresses increases steadily with age. The older our body gets, the less effective is its defence against toxins, such as free radicals, and the less efficient it becomes at repairing cell and tissue damage. This increases the likelihood that toxins will cause harm through oxidative, inflammatory and other degenerative processes. For example, the older we get the less effective our bodies are at preventing the oxidation involved in the formation of atherosclerosis; this puts older individuals at an increased risk for heart attacks and strokes. The abnormal chronic systemic inflammatory response, which underlies a number of chronic diseases, is also more likely to occur as we grow old.

An Example of Two Environmental Factors that Accelerate Aging and Cause Disease

Our skin provides an excellent, visible example of the integral relationship between aging and degenerative disease. Older individuals, and in particular women, who have smoked regularly and over a long period – thereby chronically exposing their body to myriad toxins – have much older looking skin than non-smokers of a similar age. Compared with their non-smoking counterparts, smokers also have much higher incidences of various forms of cancer, heart disease and other disorders.

Chronic exposure to ultraviolet light, usually in the form of sunlight, has a similar effect, accelerating the aging of skin cells and increasing the risk of skin cancer. Both the aging and mutagenic effects of ultraviolet light are due to its oxidative effects and free radical production. Beneath the skin, the association between aging and degenerative diseases – due to shared degenerative processes – is less visible, but just as strong.

▶ Retarding the Aging Process

There is, at present, little we can do to change the programmed mortality of our cells. And even if we eventually discover how to do so, we would need to proceed with great caution and moderation: given the potential for increasing the risk of cancer, we may do ourselves a disservice by extending cell life indefinitely. However, where we can effectively counter aging – and do so without risk to our health – is by protecting our DNA and other cellular components from toxin damage and the wear and tear to which all of us are subject to lesser or larger degrees. In doing so, we can prevent premature aging and retain good health for longer.

The range in longevity within species and between populations attests to the fact that while aging is inevitable, the rate of aging is certainly not invariable. Partly responsible for this variation are individuals' genetic differences and, in general, people with long-lived relatives tend to live longer themselves. However, environmental factors also have a strong influence on the rate of senescence. While our genes remain beyond our control, we can do much to ensure that we will live as long as they allow us to. We can achieve this by avoiding the environmental factors that are known to reduce life expectancy. These include obesity, smoking, alcohol, drugs, environmental pollutants, lack of exercise, and physical and emotional stress.

Dietary factors also play a crucial role in aging and the influence of diet on life expectancy can be either positive or negative. The excessive consumption of red meat may, for example, increase our susceptibility to some cancers like cancer of the colon; more broadly, excessive calorific intake increases general systemic stress and wear and tear on the body. Resveratrol, an antioxidant found in grapes and red wine, is one example of a phytochemical that has been found to substantially extend the lifespan of several animal species; and evidence is mounting that other phytochemicals have potent anti-aging properties too.

▶ Phytochemicals and Aging

Preventing oxidation (a key degenerative process) is one of the most effective ways in which aging can be combated and the phytochemicals in spices provide the ideal dietary means to do so. In addition to their numerous antioxidants which mop up free radicals, spices contain different classes of compounds that indirectly protect against oxidation, by stimulating and protecting other dietary and internally produced antioxidants. Another indirect antioxidant effect of phytochemicals involves dietary sugars such as glucose and fructose. These sugars can react with amino acids in a process called *glycation* that is believed to lead to accelerated aging via an oxidative process (and associated free-radical production) called *glycoxidation*. This process damages structural proteins thereby weakening many different tissue types – including those of blood vessel walls and kidneys – and reduces the production of DNA-repair enzymes. The regular intake of spices like *cinnamon* and *fenugreek* that lower blood glucose levels can help protect against excessive glycation, and the antioxidants in most spices help to counter glycoxidation and other age-related processes.

Not all of the ways in which phytochemicals slow down aging are well understood. But given the close relationship between aging and degenerative diseases, it is likely that most phytochemicals exert their retarding effect on aging via the same mechanisms responsible for their protective effects against degenerative diseases. By increasing our intake of the phytochemicals that prevent degenerative diseases, we simultaneously benefit from the deceleration of aging, helping us to look and feel younger, for longer.

CHAPTER 13

Obesity and Weight Loss

S U M M A R Y • S U M M A R Y • S U M M A R Y

☐ Obesity is a global problem with diverse and devastating health consequences.

☐ Although weight gain is essentially caused by an imbalance between energy input and energy output, there are several factors that predispose individuals to obesity.

☐ Genetics, fat absorption, metabolic rate and appetite all influence weight gain.

☐ Several spices, including *chilies, garlic, green tea* and *fenugreek*, help to prevent and combat obesity. They act by suppressing the appetite, reducing fat absorption and fat deposition, and increasing the metabolic "burning off" of fat.

Obesity is a condition in which the body's natural energy reserve, in the form of stored fat, exceeds the threshold beyond which it may have serious health consequences. In the last 50 years it has become a true global pandemic that affects both developed and developing countries alike. A particularly worrying feature of this trend is the increasing numbers of overweight and obese children, leading to a dramatic increase in childhood cases of obesity-related diseases.

Although obesity often has adverse mechanical and social consequences, by far the most serious effect of the condition is the metabolic havoc and related health problems that result from excess fat stores. These include cancer, cardiovascular disease, diabetes, arthritis and hormone imbalances. One example of such a hormonal change is the excess production of the hormone, oestrogen. Oestrogen is manufactured by certain organs as well as by adipose tissue, and the more fat cells there are the greater the quantities of oestrogen that are released into the body. Abnormally high levels of this hormone can cause a range of health problems in both men and women. Men who have too much oestrogen suffer from gynaecomastia, or enlarged breasts as well as other changes associated with this "feminizing" hormone. Overproduction of oestrogen can lead to the development of hormone-dependent cancers in both men and women. Just as the health consequences of the condition can vary depending on gender, they can also vary from individual to individual, depending on where in the body the fat is stored. Excess fat stored around the abdomen is more of a health risk than that deposited around the hips and the extremities.

A number of factors, some of which are better understood than others, can contribute to the development of obesity. These factors take effect through a range of different mechanisms but, in all cases, the consequence is the storage of surplus energy – which may enter the body as carbohydrates or fats – as excessive quantities of body fat.

The Body Mass Index

☐ An obese person is defined as someone who has a body mass index (BMI) of more than 30, while someone with a BMI of between 25 and 30 would be considered to be 'overweight'.
☐ The BMI of an individual is calculated by dividing his height in metres by the square of his weight in kilograms.
☐ There is very little evidence to show that people who are only a few BMI points overweight are more at risk of disease than those who have a BMI below 25.

▶ Fat Metabolism and the Causes of Obesity

Fat deposition is a defensive mechanism that enables the storage of energy when food is abundant, thereby increasing the chances of survival during times of food scarcity and famine. In earlier times those individuals who were efficient at storing fat were more likely to survive food

111

HOW SPICES INHIBIT DISEASE PROCESSES

shortages, and fat storage was especially valuable in pregnant and lactating women due to their higher than normal energy requirements. Unfortunately, during modern times of plenty we still retain this innate capacity to store fat and what was once an advantage for the efficient energy accumulators has now become a health risk for them.

Viewed simplistically, obesity is caused by too much energy intake, in the form of food, and not enough energy output, in the form of basic metabolic processes and exercise. However, the reasons that so many of us become overweight or obese are a little more complex than this straightforward equation suggests. Although a sedentary lifestyle and the availability of cheap, high-energy carbohydrate and fat-laden foods are the principal causes of obesity, there are sometimes other aggravating factors to consider. These are diverse and include a genetic pre-disposition; lifestyle-related factors such as stress and sleep deprivation; psychological problems that manifest themselves as eating disorders; underlying illness; certain medications; a diet dominated by high glycaemic index foods; and habitual dieting with its attendant weight fluctuation. It has been suggested recently that certain virus infections can increase a tendency to put on weight.

In many cases these factors work by interfering with our appetite control mechanisms, which are partially responsible for the maintenance of normal weight.

▶ Appetite Control

The failure of appetite control is often directly responsible for obesity and can exacerbate and entrench the condition once it has developed. Satiety control mechanisms may also be dampened as a consequence of obesity which has been caused by other factors. A number of mechanisms are involved in this complex regulatory system, and a malfunction of any one of these may result in the consumption of excess food.

The senses of smell and taste are two of the most important of the appetite control mechanisms. When we smell or eat food, receptors in the nose are stimulated by food odour molecules and convey these signals to the satiety centre in the brain. By monitoring the intensity of these signals, the satiety centre is able to gauge when we have had enough to eat. As a result, individuals who have a poor sense of smell or who suffer from a complete loss of the sense of smell tend to eat more than those with a normal sense of smell. Unsurprisingly, strongly flavoured and seasoned foods – which often owe this property to spices – stimulate the satiety centre far more effectively than bland foods, and we tend to eat less of the former as a result.

Distention of the stomach by food also induces the release of hormones that act as appetite suppressants and some foods, particularly the spices, have the same effects, even in the absence of stomach distention. A group of hormones called adipokines which are produced by fat tissue are also thought to play an important role in appetite regulation. Adipokines include the hormone, leptin, which is generally released in direct proportion to the amount of fat stored in the body, thereby helping the brain to gauge when there is a dearth or an excess of fat. Some obese individuals, however, appear to have genetic or other problems that impede the normal appetite-regulating effects of leptin.

Anti-Obesity Properties of Key Spices	
Anorectics (appetite suppressants)	*Capsicum, garlic, green tea*
Increase metabolic rate	*Capsicum, garlic, green tea*
Reduce fat absorption	*Fenugreek, garlic, ginger, green tea*
Reduces conversion of glucose to fat	*Green tea*

▶ Spices and Obesity

Spices have a number of properties that make them effective agents to help prevent and treat obesity. In their role as appetite suppressants, spices are known to work in three principal ways. The strong odours and flavours common to all spices rapidly stimulate the satiety centre in the brain, thereby diminishing feelings of hunger. Certain spices, such as *chilies*, act by simulating the release of appetite suppressing hormones in the intestine. *Garlic* and *green tea* meanwhile reduce the appetite by increasing the brain's sensitivity to leptin.

Another important anti-obesity property of spices is an ability to stimulate the nervous system to release hormones like adrenalin. These hormones speed up the metabolic rate which, in turn, helps "burn off" surplus fat. *Capsicums* (including *chilies* and *red peppers*), *garlic* and *green tea* have all been shown to increase the metabolic rate, in some cases by up to 10 percent. Clinical trials have demonstrated that these spices can be effective both in protecting against weight gain and assisting in weight loss. In the capsicum family, more than one phytochemical is known to be responsible for this effect: capsaicin (found in high amounts in chilies) and the less spicy capsiate (found in the milder paprika and red peppers) both increase metabolic rate. Some spices, including *ginger*, *fenugreek*, *garlic* and *green tea*, reduce the absorption of fat from the intestines. Green tea acts by antagonizing the conversion of glucose into fat while enhancing its conversion into muscle glycogen.

The diverse ways in which spices act provide the ideal combination of tools with which to help prevent weight gain and fight obesity. In conjunction with a sensible weight loss programme, they are valuable adjuncts for us to use in the global fight against obesity.

Chronic Systemic Inflammation

CHAPTER 14

SUMMARY • SUMMARY • SUMMARY

☐ Chronic systemic inflammation (CSI) is a low-grade, pervasive form of inflammation that damages the endothelial linings of arteries and is a cause of *insulin resistance*. It has also been implicated in damage to a variety of other tissues and organs.

☐ CSI may be caused by a number of factors including obesity, infection, toxins and autoimmune diseases, and it can lead to several other chronic diseases, including atherosclerosis, obesity and diabetes.

☐ Disorders associated with CSI typically exhibit immune dysfunction, oxidative stress and free-radical production. The phytochemicals found in spices can reduce the pathological effects of CSI by acting against each of these contributory factors as well as by direct anti-inflammatory action.

☐ The most powerful anti-inflammatory spices include *bay leaf, black pepper, garlic, ginger, green tea, oregano, rosemary, thyme* and *turmeric*.

Inflammation is the immune system's response to infection, injury and chemical or physical irritation. Broadly divided into acute and chronic forms, inflammation is one of the body's essential defence mechanisms and plays a vital role in protecting us against microbial attack, external and internally-produced toxins, as well as damaged and diseased cells and tissues.

The inflammatory response is a multifaceted, highly complex collection of processes that depend on the coordinated action of a variety of different cells and molecules. The most important components involved in the inflammatory response include several types of specialised immune cells, platelets, antibodies, chemical messengers called interleukins and cytokines, and other chemicals like histamine and prostaglandins. One of the important effects of inflammation is to increase the permeability of blood vessels, allowing blood plasma to escape into the tissues and organs. The increased permeability improves access for the immune cells to damaged and infected tissues, thereby facilitating the destruction and removal of damaged and diseased cells. Unfortunately, this process is inherently destructive, and both acute and chronic inflammation may cause damage to healthy tissues.

Typically, the longer the inflammatory process lasts, the more damage it does to the tissues involved. In the case of a local infection, inflammatory damage often manifests itself as scar tissue and if a wound becomes infected or fails to heal quickly, it will leave more scar tissue than it would have had it healed normally. Similar but less visible processes are at work in a lower grade form of this process called *chronic systemic inflammation*. This type of inflammation can cause widespread damage to a range of different tissue types that ultimately leads to specific disease entities.

▶ Chronic Systemic Inflammation and Disease

Chronic systemic inflammation (CSI) is a low-grade, pervasive form of inflammation with potentially devastating consequences. The inflammatory reactions characteristic of CSI are less severe than those seen in acute inflammatory responses. However, CSI has been implicated as a major causative factor for several serious chronic diseases. From this perspective, it is one of the most dangerous – if insidious – types of inflammation.

Although CSI and local inflammation share the same biochemical processes, CSI is not restricted to a specific tissue or organ, but instead involves the endothelial lining of blood vessels and several other tissue types. As a result the disruptive effects of CSI are far reaching, causing damage to the nervous, endocrine and other systems. This damage may, in turn, precipitate or exacerbate a wide variety of other pathological processes. CSI is, for example, closely implicated in the development of insulin resistance – and thereby metabolic syndrome and diabetes –

which is rarely found without raised levels of the circulating inflammatory markers associated with CSI. Damage to the arterial endothelium and the subsequent development of atherosclerosis has also been linked to CSI. In addition to its important underlying role in obesity, insulin resistance and atherosclerosis, CSI has also been implicated in some forms of depression and even sleep disorders.

Only recently identified and subjected to scientific investigation, CSI is still considered to be more of an underlying pathological process rather than a particular disease entity, and there are no specific diagnostic tests or targeted treatment interventions for it. Although the precise causes of CSI are currently not clear, a number of factors have been implicated in the condition.

Table 5: Causes of Chronic Systemic Inflammation

Obesity
Several substances involved in the inflammatory response are produced in adipose tissue. Abdominal fat in particular is very active both metabolically and immunologically, and is associated with the production of pro-inflammatory cytokines, C-reactive protein and other circulating markers of inflammation. Obesity and the accumulation of abdominal fat leads to abnormally high levels of these substances, causing imbalances to the immune system and the increase of the inflammatory response.

Infections
All chronic infections sustain the inflammatory response by stimulating an increase in the production of pro-inflammatory cytokines. When present in excessive amounts, these chemical messengers are capable of prompting antibodies and white blood cells to destroy cells that may be healthy and far-removed from the site of the primary infection. Infections that could contribute to CSI include undiagnosed kidney or bladder infections, low-grade gall bladder infection, chronic tonsillitis, diverticular disease, hepatitis, chronic viral diseases like HIV, cytomegalovirus and infectious mononucleosis or any other chronic infection such as Lyme disease or brucellosis. Periodontal disease, in particular, has been closely linked to CSI.

117

Periodontal Disease

Along with obesity, periodontal disease (or periodontal infection) is believed to be one of the major causes of CSI. Dental plaque is often responsible for initiating periodontal disease by releasing a variety of biologically active products, such as bacterial and protein toxins, and organic acids. These molecules stimulate the body to produce pro-inflammatory cytokines, prostaglandins and other molecules involved in inflammation. All of these can contribute to a low-grade CSI in tissues far from the mouth. The treatment of periodontal disease substantially reduces the quantities of circulating pro-inflammatory agents, and can even reverse some of the damage done to the endothelial lining of the arteries.

Intestinal Parasites

Intestinal parasites such as giardia, roundworms, hookworms and others set up potent inflammatory responses in the lining of the intestines resulting in the release of inflammatory products into the blood stream. These substances can, in turn, contribute to CSI.

Environmental Toxins, Drugs and Tobacco

Most foreign substances can trigger an inflammatory response. This is probably one of the reasons that smoking tobacco is associated with an increased risk for heart disease and stroke. Inflammation in response to tobacco toxins is known to cause damage to the arterial endothelium, thereby aggravating the development of atherosclerosis.

Allergies and Autoimmune Disease

Allergies and autoimmune diseases are pathological conditions where the immune system reacts inappropriately to normal tissues or non-threatening environmental substances like pollens. These conditions, which include rheumatoid arthritis and lupus, vary widely in their intensity. However, particularly in the case of autoimmune disease, they may precipitate serious inflammatory-mediated tissue damage. There is, moreover, some evidence to show that periodontal disease and other chronic infections may actually initiate some allergies and autoimmune disorders, thereby contributing both directly and indirectly to CSI.

▶ Spices and CSI

The first step in dealing with CSI is to find and treat the cause of the inflammation. This may require improving dental hygiene, stopping smoking, avoiding allergens, or losing weight. Such interventions can be dramatically augmented by the consumption of spices, several of which have powerful anti-inflammatory effects. Among the most potent of these are *bay leaf, garlic, ginger, oregano, rosemary, thyme* and *turmeric.* The anti-inflammatory phytochemicals contained in these spices act on a variety of mechanisms including the inhibition of COX-I and COX-2 enzymes and chemicals such as prostaglandins that are all important components of the inflammatory response.[1]

Other spices, in particular *black pepper, garlic* and *green tea,* counteract CSI by modulating the immune system thereby limiting the excessive production of pro-inflammatory cytokines. Furthermore, as many of the causes of CSI – including obesity, toxins and infections – are associated with oxidative stress, the antioxidants found in most spices help control this condition too. The myriad spice-derived antioxidants are able to "mop up" a wide range of inhaled, ingested and internally produced free radicals that can lead to CSI. Indirectly, spices' antimicrobial phyto-chemicals can also fight CSI, by protecting against the infections that precipitate this inflammatory response. In short, spice-derived phyto-chemicals have all the attributes required to minimise the impact on our health of the insidious, destructive and potentially lethal effects of CSI.

Anti-inflammatory Properties of Key Spices

Direct anti-inflammatory action	*Bay leaf, garlic, ginger, oregano, rosemary thyme, turmeric*
Immune modulation and control of pro-inflammatory cytokines	*Black pepper, garlic, green tea*
Protect against lipid oxidation associated with inflammation	*Allspice, cinnamon, clove, ginger, oregano, peppermint, sage, thyme*

---

1 The consumption of these spices will not reduce the beneficial effects of a normal inflammatory response.

CHAPTER 15

Salicylates

S U M M A R Y • S U M M A R Y • S U M M A R Y

☐ Salicylates, including aspirin and several similar compounds, are a valuable group of antioxidant phytochemicals that are found in many spices.

☐ In addition to their potent anti-inflammatory properties, salicylates lower the risk of cardiovascular disease by reducing platelet stickiness. New research suggests that they also protect against cancer and Alzheimer's disease.

☐ Salicylate-containing spices include *allspice, bay leaf, capsicum, cardamom, caraway, cinnamon, fenugreek, garlic, ginger, liquorice, nutmeg, onion, soy, tarragon* and *turmeric.*

The salicylates belong to an interesting group of compounds that includes one of our most common synthetic drugs, aspirin, in addition to its natural counterpart and several similar phytochemicals. They are very good examples of compounds that have several applications in both the prevention and treatment of several degenerative diseases. It is for these reasons that they are discussed in more detail than the other phytochemicals mentioned in this book.

Salicylates belong to a valuable class of closely related antioxidant compounds that includes several phytochemicals. The most important members of this group are *salicylic acid* and *acetylsalicylic acid* that occur in several common fruits and vegetables, and are particularly abundant in many spices. Acetylsalicylic acid is the chemical name for aspirin and, although it was originally extracted from willow tree bark, it is now chemically synthesised. *Methyl salicylate* is the active ingredient in oil of wintergreen that is used as a topical treatment for joint, muscle and other inflamed tissues. It was originally extracted from the box berry (creeping wintergreen) plant and is still used to flavour root beer and chewing gum.

SALICYLATES

Aspirin is well established as a valuable drug, particularly with respect to cardiovascular disease and a number of inflammatory disorders. More recently it has been found to have protective effects against some cancers and Alzheimer's disease. Similarly, plant-derived salicylates have anti-inflammatory, antioxidant and other attributes. In this way they make a significant contribution to the increased longevity and decreased risk of chronic diseases that are associated with a diet rich in fruit and vegetables.

Spices Containing Salicyclates	
Allspice	Bay leaf
Capsicum	Cardamon
Caraway	Cinnamon
Fenugreek	Garlic
Ginger	Liquorice
Nutmeg	Onion
Soy	Tarragon
Turmeric	

Medicinal Properties

▶ Cancer

Salicylates have been shown to protect against several types of cancer. Most research investigating this prophylactic effect has focused on cancer of the colon. This occurred after epidemiological studies pointed to the low incidence of this cancer among individuals who regularly took aspirin (or other non-steroidal anti-inflammatory medicines) to treat other unrelated diseases. It is, however, likely that this research interest will expand, as new epidemiological findings suggest that salicylates are valuable prophylactic agents for other cancers too. One very recent study,

121

for example, shows that people who take more than two aspirin per week for several years reduce their chances of developing skin cancer by more than 50 percent.

Salicylates appear to inhibit tumour formation through at least two different mechanisms. In colon cancer cells, they have been shown to induce cell cycle arrest by activating a tumour-suppressing protein that plays an important role in inducing apoptosis. Some salicylates also activate the cytokine TNF-alpha, which is a powerful initiator of apoptosis in certain cancer cell lines, and salicylic acid can also stimulate apoptosis in cancer cells by inhibiting the tumour promoting cytokine, NF-κB.

▶ Cardiovascular Disease

Low dose aspirin is used extensively in patients with cardiovascular disease to prevent platelet aggregation and reduce the risk of heart attacks and thrombotic strokes. It also plays an important role in the treatment of heart attacks by preventing clot formation at the site of a ruptured atheromatous plaque. Interestingly, fruit, vegetables and spices can provide us with at least 75 milligrams of natural salicylates per day if we eat sufficient quantities of these foods. Seventy-five milligrams is the amount of low dose aspirin typically taken by patients who are at risk of developing heart attack or thrombotic stroke. Vegetarians, who generally eat more vegetables and fruit than omnivores, tend to ingest enough of these foods to provide themselves with 75 milligrams or more of naturally occurring aspirin. Those individuals who eat large quantities of spices every day provide themselves with similar amounts of salicylates.

▶ Anti-inflammatory Effects

Aspirin (acetylsalicylic acid), salicylic acid and wintergreen (methyl salicylate) have been used for centuries to treat pain and inflammatory conditions like arthritis. Recent research has shown that different types of salicylates have somewhat different mechanisms of action. For instance, acetylsalicylic acid works primarily by inhibiting the pro-inflammatory

COX-1 enzyme but has a weaker effect on the COX-2 enzyme that stimulates the production of pro-inflammatory prostaglandins. (Newer non-steroidal anti-inflammatory drugs called COX-2 inhibitors have been developed to specifically target the COX-2 enzyme and are considered more effective than aspirin in controlling pain and inflammation.) Salicylic acid, on the other hand, has no effect on either the COX-1 or COX-2 enzymes. However, its anti-inflammatory property is due to its direct action on the cells where it inhibits the production of pro-inflammatory prostaglandins.

▶ Alzheimer's Disease

A growing body of evidence shows that those individuals taking aspirin over a long period of time have lower than average incidences of Alzheimer's disease and other neurodegenerative conditions. The mechanisms underlying this protective effect have yet to be established, but Alzheimer's disease is known to have an inflammatory component. The anti-inflammatory and antioxidant properties of aspirin are probably responsible for this prophylactic effect, and we can safely assume that naturally occurring acetylsalicylic acid and other salicylates have the same protective effects.

Note on Medicinal Use

Medicinal aspirin is associated with side effects like indigestion and intestinal bleeding and should be avoided when certain other medications are prescribed or if there are other contraindications to its use. However, salicylates in foods and spices have not been shown to have any of these effects.

On the other hand a very small number of people do have allergies or intolerances to all salicylates both in their synthetic and natural forms. These individuals should avoid foods that contain significant quantities of salicylates.

PART 3

DISEASE-
PREVENTING
PROPERTIES
OF INDIVIDUAL
SPICES

Turmeric
Curcuma longa

CHAPTER 16

Anticancer, anti-Alzheimer's, anti-inflammatory, chelating agent

The root of *Curcuma longa* is ground up to provide the yellow dye and flavoured powder known as haldi in India, and turmeric in the West. Turmeric is cultivated and produced in several countries in south-eastern Asia and is used widely in Asian and Indian dishes: as a colourant for rice, a standard constituent of curry and as an inexpensive substitute for saffron. Turmeric's most important phytochemical, curcumin, is often added to food products as a colouring and to prevent their spoilage by oxidation. Herbalists prescribe it to prevent heart disease and cancer, and to treat HIV infection and arthritis. An increasing body of scientific research is showing turmeric to be one of the most valuable medicinal spices with potent preventive and, in some cases, therapeutic effects against a variety of serious chronic diseases.

Important Phytochemicals

Antioxidants: Caffeic acid, camphene, coumaric acid, curcumin, eugenol, gamma terpinene, protocatechuic acid, salicylates, tetrahydrocurcumin, turmerin, turmeronol, vanillic acid

Others: Curcumol, curdione, turmerone, zingiberene

Medicinal Properties

▶ Cancer

Turmeric's main constituent phytochemical, curcumin, is one of the most remarkable and most studied of all the spice compounds. In addition to its other medicinal properties, curcumin is an extremely valuable chemoprotective agent. Much of the research and interest in curcumin has centred on breast cancer, but it has also been found to have protective effects against cancers of the bladder, stomach, uterus and cervix. When measured against other phytochemicals that protect against cancer, curcumin exhibits at least a ten times greater chemoprotective potency than its closest rival. *In vitro* studies have shown that a single dose of curcumin inhibits cancer cell proliferation for over six days following its administration.

Curcumin is known to protect against cancer through the following mechanisms.

☐ *Tumour suppression:* Curcumin assists the body's natural tumour-suppressing mechanisms in a number of different ways.
☐ *Cancer cell death:* Curcumin destroys cancer cells both directly, by stimulating apoptosis, and indirectly, by inhibiting telomerase activity, thereby terminating the immortality so typical of cancer cell lines.
☐ *Inhibition of tumour proliferation:* Curcumin halts tumour proliferation by inhibiting DNA synthesis in the cancer cells and disrupting their mitotic replication.
☐ *Inhibition of angiogenesis:* By inhibiting the transcription capabilities of at least two major angiogenesis-inducing factors, curcumin halts the formation of the new blood vessels that are essential for tumour growth.
☐ *Anti-oestrogenic effects:* One of turmeric's most promising uses is in the prevention and treatment of breast cancer. Most breast cancers are hormone dependent, requiring oestrogen as a growth stimulant. Tamoxifen, which is one of the most used drugs in the treatment of breast cancer, works against this hormone-mediated process, interfering with oestrogen's tumour stimulating effects. Curcumin exhibits its anti-oestrogenic effects by blocking the oestrogen-dependent receptors on tumour cells, thereby interrupting the stimulatory effects of oestrogen and slowing tumour

growth. Some studies have shown that curcumin may be at least as effective as tamoxifen as an oestrogen antagonist, with none of the attendant side effects of this drug.

Some of the other phytochemicals found in turmeric are also known to have chemoprotective effects. Therefore, when it comes to prevention, it is better to take the parent spice, turmeric, rather than the pure curcumin extract. However, the treatment of existing breast cancer may call for more specific dosages of curcumin, the administration of which would need to be supervised by a qualified health practitioner.

▶ Alzheimer's (AD) and Parkinson's Diseases

Curcumin exhibits several properties that make it a valuable preventive agent for these two devastating and increasingly common diseases. Recent research, moreover, suggests that curcumin may also be able to *reverse* Alzheimer's disease. Thus, although turmeric is probably most effective as a preventive agent against these illnesses, it may also help by improving cognitive problems and preventing further deterioration of existing disease.

Curcumin works against these neurodegenerative diseases via the following mechanisms.

☐ *Inhibition of inflammation and oxidation:* The accumulation of amyloid protein in the brain is an important factor associated with Alzheimer's disease. Its deposition is associated with oxidative damage and inflammation in the brain tissues, and there is evidence that the risk of developing AD can be reduced by increased consumption of phytochemicals with antioxidant and anti-inflammatory properties (aspirin and other non-steroidal anti-inflammatory drugs are also thought to protect against AD). Curcumin is both a potent antioxidant and anti-inflammatory agent and has been shown to suppress oxidative damage, inflammation and the deposition of damaging amyloid protein in the brain. Exciting new *in vitro* research has also shown that curcumin can actually disaggregate existing amyloid plaques and, in so doing, may reverse the course of the disease.

☐ *Removal of toxic metals:* Another cause of amyloid deposition in the brain is thought to be due to certain metals, as higher concentrations of harmful metals have been found in the brains of AD sufferers than in non-AD individuals. Metal molecules that find their way into the brain can both induce amyloid aggregation and have direct toxic effects on brain cells. Certain chelating agents have shown promise in the treatment of Alzheimer's disease and curcumin's chelating properties enable it to assist the body in the removal of potentially toxic metals from the brain and other tissues.

☐ *Prevention of abnormal brain cell proliferation:* The abnormal proliferation of the brain's non-neuronal cells, microglia, neuroglia and astrocytes, is another pathological process that is associated with the development of both Alzheimer's and Parkinson's diseases. Curcumin has been shown to prevent the proliferation of these cells which, if allowed to continue growing, cause damage to the brain's neuronal tissue. Interestingly, the action of curcumin in this context is not dose dependent; the sustained intake of small quantities is more effective than larger doses taken over a short time span.

▶ **Inflammatory Diseases**

With its powerful combination of anti-oxidative and anti-inflammatory properties, turmeric is one of the most valuable spices for the prevention and treatment of disorders like arthritis and other inflammatory and autoimmune diseases. Turmeric has been used for millennia in Ayurveda and other traditional medical systems and is considered a stalwart in the treatment of these diseases. Much of its anti-inflammatory potency can be attributed to curcumin which is both an effective COX-2 inhibitor as well as a strong antioxidant. However, other phytochemicals found in turmeric, in particular the salicylates, also make a valuable contribution to its anti-inflammatory activities and thereby its preventive properties against arthritis and autoimmune disorders.

❱ Chelation

Copper and iron are both essential nutrients but if they accumulate in excessive quantities they can cause serious and sometimes irreversible oxidative damage to a variety of tissues in the body. They also induce the activity of NF-κB, a cytokine associated with inflammation of many tissue types. Curcumin is a powerful chelating agent for both metals, binding to the metal ions and allowing them to be safely excreted in the urine.

Cinnamon

CHAPTER **17**

Cinnamomum zeylanicum

Antidiabetic, blood lipid control, potent antioxidant

Cinnamon is a spice obtained from the bark of *Cinnamomum zeylanicum*, a tree that is indigenous to Sri Lanka and now cultivated in several other tropical countries too. It is often confused with the "other cinnamon,"[1] a product derived from the tree *Cinnamomum aromaticum*, that has a similar flavour and medicinal properties to "true" cinnamon. Both of these spices are widely available in most countries.

Cinnamon was used by the ancient Egyptians along with other spices in their embalming and mummification of the dead, its anti-bacterial and antioxidant properties assisting in the preservation of the bodies. It has also been used as a traditional medicine to treat a variety of ailments including colds and digestive problems, as a perfume, and for flavouring wines. Today cinnamon is used primarily as flavouring for confectionery and as a fashionable spice in tea and coffee. Intense medical interest has, however, been stimulated by the recent discovery of its potent antidiabetic effects. This property has been attributed to hydroxychalcone and other polyphenols found in cinnamon (e.g. caffeic acid, isoeugenol, proanthocyanidins) that also have antioxidant and lipid-lowering properties.

Important Phytochemicals

Antioxidants: Caffeic acid, camphene, coumaric acid, epicatechin, gamma-terpinene, isoeugenol, linalyl-acetate, mannitol, methyl-eugenol, myrcene, phenol, proanthocyanidins, vanillin

Others: Cinnamaldehyde, cinnamic acid esters, coumarin, eugenol, hydroxychalcone, safrole, salicylates

---

1 *Cinnamomum aromaticum* is also known as Cassia, Chinese Cinnamon or Chinese Cassia. In their whole forms they are easy to tell apart but when sold as a powder they look and taste similar.

132

Medicinal Properties

❱ Diabetes

Cinnamon is a powerful inducer of insulin sensitivity making it an effective treatment for both Type II diabetes and metabolic syndrome. In these conditions, cell receptors become insensitive to insulin, making it difficult for glucose to enter the cell. This leads to cell starvation and high blood sugar levels which are responsible for the dire health consequences associated with these diseases. Cinnamon enhances the activity of the enzymes that increase cell receptor insulin sensitivity, and inhibits those that have the opposite effect. Recent landmark clinical trials have shown that the daily addition of as little as one gram of cinnamon to the diet leads to a reduction of blood glucose levels of between 18 percent and 29 percent in Type II diabetics. This impressive drop in blood sugar levels is a gradual process, taking up to 40 days to occur, but it is also long-lasting. When the diabetic patients on the trial (whose blood glucose levels had dropped to normal) stopped taking the cinnamon, these lower levels were sustained for up to 20 days. This suggests that cinnamon has the effect of gradually changing the cellular response to insulin and, in so doing, avoids the wide fluctuations of insulin and blood sugar levels that lead to the dangerous episodes of hyperglycaemia and hypoglycaemia commonly seen in poorly controlled diabetes. In this context it is notable that, even if cinnamon is not taken every day, one does not see the dangerous fluctuations of blood glucose levels associated with erratic ingestion of oral antidiabetic medication

Cinnamon has the additional benefit of lowering blood lipids, which is an important means of controlling the disease. Diabetics have a higher than average risk of developing hypertension, stroke and heart disease, and it is essential to rigorously control the blood pressure, cholesterol and triglyceride levels in these patients. There are no contemporary anti-diabetic drugs that lower both blood sugar *and* blood lipids. Therefore, in addition to their diabetic medicines, diabetics generally have to take one of the statin drugs to keep their cholesterol, lipoprotein and triglyceride levels normal. Cinnamon, however, provides all these properties in a single package. It is, moreover, a powerful antioxidant which is beneficial in Type II diabetes, as many sufferers are overweight and under constant oxidative stress.

▶ Cardiovascular Disease and Blood Lipids

Cinnamon has a powerful effect on abnormally high blood lipid levels. The same clinical trials mentioned in the previous section also showed that Type II diabetics who took as little as one gram of cinnamon daily for more than 40 days experienced a substantial improvement in their blood lipid profiles. Cholesterol levels declined by 13 percent to 26 percent, triglyceride levels plummeted by between 23 percent to 30 percent, and LDL levels sank by between 10 percent to 24 percent. Interestingly the levels of HDL, which is a beneficial lipoprotein, remained constant. As in the case of glucose, the improved blood lipid levels were sustained for a period of up to 20 days after cessation of the cinnamon treatment. These impressive figures are easily comparable with the most effective statin drugs on the market. Cinnamon can also help non-diabetics with high blood lipid levels to reduce the risk of developing heart disease and stroke.

▶ Antioxidant Properties

Cinnamon contains some of the most varied and potent antioxidants of all plants, making it an important food in the control of oxidative stress and thereby the wide range of chronic diseases that are associated with oxidative damage.

Black pepper
Piper nigrum

CHAPTER 18

Anticancer, antioxidant, immunomodulator, bioavailability enhancer

Black pepper is derived from the fruit of a climbing vine native to southern India and Sri Lanka. White pepper is likewise made from this fruit but is processed differently. Used almost universally, black pepper is one of the most common condiments worldwide and figures prominently in most curry recipes. It is also frequently included in the prescriptions of Ayurvedic and other traditional health practitioners. The spicy tang of black pepper is due to its most important and well-researched phytochemical, piperine.

Important Phytochemicals

Antioxidants: Caffeic acid, camphene, carvacrol, coumaric acid, eugenol, gamma terpinene, hyperoside, isoquercitrin, kaempferol, linalyl acetate, methyl eugenol, myrcene, myristicin, quercetin, quercitrin, rhamnetin, rutin, ubiquinone

Others: α-pinene, bisabolone, borneol, carvonecineol, caryophyllene, caryophyllene oxide, humulene, limonene, linalool, phellandrene, pinenes, piperine, sabinene, terpinene

---

Medicinal Properties

❯ Cancer

By increasing the bioavailability of other anti-tumourigenic spices, black pepper dramatically increases their potency and effectiveness against cancer. In addition to this important property, black pepper also counteracts cancer development directly. Its principal phytochemical, piperine,

135

inhibits some of the pro-inflammatory cytokines that are produced by tumour cells. In so doing it interferes with the signalling mechanisms between cancer cells, thereby reducing the chances of tumour progression. Collectively, these properties make black pepper one of the most important spices for preventing cancer.

▶ Oxidative Stress

Black pepper contains several powerful antioxidants and is thus one of the most important spices for preventing and curtailing oxidative stress. In addition to their direct antioxidant properties, several of these compounds work indirectly by enhancing the action of other antioxidants. This makes black pepper particularly valuable in minimising the damage caused by a diet rich in saturated fats, one of the main causes of oxidative stress. The high levels of cholesterol and triglycerides associated with oxidative stress inhibit the efficacy of important antioxidants like glutathione, superoxide dismutase, catalase, glutathione peroxidase, vitamin C and vitamin E. However, in the face of this potentially destructive process, black pepper actually maintains and enhances the levels and efficacy of these important antioxidant compounds.

▶ Immunomodulation

Black pepper exhibits immunomodulatory properties and is capable of boosting the number and the efficacy of white cells, thereby assisting the body to mount a very powerful defence against invading microbes and cancer cells.

▶ Bioavailability Enhancement

Piperine increases the bioavailability of valuable phytochemicals present in other spices and can boost the activity of biochemically active compounds contained in green tea, curcumin and a variety of other spices by up to several hundred percent, depending on the molecule concerned. It does this via two principal mechanisms. First, it promotes the rapid absorption of certain chemicals from the gastrointestinal tract, protecting them from being broken down by chemicals in the intestinal lumen and by enzymes that occur in the cells lining the intestines. Secondly, once the compound has entered the blood stream, piperine provides protection against oxidative damage by liver enzymes. In this way black pepper enables us to reap optimum benefits from the medicinal phytochemicals found in other dietary spices.

Note on Medicinal Use

Piperine is now being sold in formulas with other spice extracts, such as curcumin, principally to enhance the bioavailability of these other molecules. However, as evident from the above list of phytochemicals, piperine is not the only biologically active substance found in this spice. Many of its other constituent compounds are the same as those derived from other plants with proven health benefits. One can confidently assume therefore, that those found in black pepper exhibit similar beneficial effects, even if they have not yet been studied in the context of this spice. To obtain the full *protective* benefits of black pepper it is therefore advisable to take the whole spice rather than piperine alone, unless the latter is being used in combination with other compounds to *treat* a specific disease.

CHAPTER 19

Ginger

Zingiber officinale

Anticancer, cardioprotective, antidiabetic, anti-Alzheimer's disease, anti-obesity, anti-inflammatory, antimicrobial

One of the most popular of all the spices, ginger is derived from the root of a plant indigenous to Asia which is now cultivated across the globe for use in an enormous variety of foods, drinks and traditional medicines. It is added to sweet and savoury dishes, condiments, confectioneries, sweets, and is a component of many traditional cuisines, including Chinese, Indian, Japanese and Thai. It has also been used in perfumes, cosmetics and is a valued medicinal plant. It is used in folk medicine to treat colds and influenza and is an effective anti-emetic used in the treatment of both motion sickness, and the nausea and vomiting associated with pregnancy. Numerous studies investigating ginger's medicinal properties have also shown it to be effective in the prevention and treatment of many of our more serious chronic degenerative diseases.

Important Phytochemicals

Antioxidants: Caffeic acid, camphene, capsaicin, chlorogenic acid, coumaric acid, curcumin, delphinidin, eugenol, ferulic acid, gingerdiol, gingerol, isoeugenol, kaempferol, melatonin, myrcene, myricetin, quercetin, shogaol, vanillic acid, vanillin, zingerone

Others: Geranial, neral, paradol, phellandrene, zerumbone, zinziberene

Medicinal Properties

▶ Cancer

Several phytochemicals found in ginger have demonstrated strong anti-cancer activities in both laboratory and clinical studies. While ginger's anti-tumourigenic effects have yet to be fully understood, they are thought to involve the following mechanisms:

- ☐ *Anti-inflammatory:* Cancer is often associated with inflammatory processes and ginger's potent anti-inflammatory activity reduces the risk of inflammation-induced malignancy. Ginger is an effective COX-2 inhibitor, curtailing the activity of potentially damaging COX-2 enzymes, the overproduction of which may cause harm to several tissue types.
- ☐ *Cancer cell death:* The pungent vanilloids, *gingerol* and *paradol* found in ginger, are very effective in killing cancer cells. They achieve this both by direct cytotoxic activity against the tumour and indirectly by inducing apoptosis in the cancer cells.
- ☐ *Reducing tumour initiation and growth:* The phytochemical *zerumbone* antagonises the processes of both tumour initiation and promotion. It does this by inducing antioxidant enzymes and by weakening the pro-inflammatory signalling pathways associated with communication between cancer cells.
- ☐ *Prevents DNA damage:* Melatonin is an antioxidant produced by the body that is also found in some plants, such as ginger. It has the valuable property of being able to access most parts of the body, including brain and nervous tissue, and protects DNA against carcinogenic free-radical damage.
- ☐ *Antibacterial:* Ginger can eliminate all strains of *Helicobacter pylori*, the bacteria that are responsible for the majority of peptic ulcers, gastritis and stomach cancer.

❱ Cardiovascular Disease and Blood Lipids

Ginger has been shown to lower dangerously high cholesterol and triglyceride levels, while raising the levels of beneficial HDL. These lipid-modulating effects are partly due to the inhibition of fat absorption from the intestines. In addition, ginger's cardioprotective effects are enhanced by its ability to reduce platelet stickiness and in so doing further reduce the risk of heart attacks and thrombotic strokes.

❱ Diabetes

Although there has been relatively little investigation into the antidiabetic properties of ginger, promising early studies show that it can increase insulin sensitivity. This suggests that, in all likelihood, it is a valuable prophylactic spice against this disease.

❱ Alzheimer's Disease

Two of ginger's most important antioxidants, *curcumin* and *gingerol*, have been shown to inhibit and even reverse the deposition in the brain of the amyloid plaques that are associated with Alzheimer's disease. Moreover, *zingerone*, another of ginger's antioxidants, neutralizes the powerful oxidant, peroxynitrite, which has also been implicated as an aggravating factor in Alzheimer's and other neurodegenerative diseases.

❱ Obesity

Ginger has a dual anti-obesity effect. The phytochemicals *gingerol* and *shogaol* increase the metabolic rate and thus help to "burn off" excessive fat. They also help to suppress the absorption of calorie-dense dietary fats from the intestines.

▶ Antioxidant Effects

Ginger is a source of a large number of important antioxidants that, amongst other activities, reduce lipid oxidation by enhancing the activities of crucial internally produced antioxidants, such as superoxide dismutase. *Melatonin*, in particular, is not only a highly effective free-radical scavenger itself, but also stimulates production of the main antioxidant enzyme of the brain, glutathione peroxidase.

▶ Anti-inflammatory Properties

Ginger's long-valued role as a treatment for arthritis and other inflammatory conditions has now been substantiated by a number of scientific studies that show how it is involved in several anti-inflammatory mechanisms. It is a strong inhibitor of COX-2 enzymes, pro-inflammatory cytokines and prostaglandins that are all important components of the inflammatory response. Abnormal tissue inflammation occurs when an excess of prostaglandins, cytokines and COX-2 enzymes are released by cells in joint tissue. The more of these molecules that are released, the more inflammatory cells and chemicals are attracted to the joints where they cause pain and damage to the joint surfaces. These substances are integral to inflammatory mechanisms that can involve many tissue types, as well as the condition known as chronic systemic inflammation.

Several modern COX-2 inhibitor drugs are used to treat arthritis and other painful inflammatory diseases. These were developed in an attempt to replace the older non-steroidal anti-inflammatory drugs such as ibuprofen and indomethacin, which can have serious side effects including stomach ulceration and bleeding. Unfortunately, although the newer drugs do have fewer side effects, there is some evidence that they may aggravate cardiovascular disease and precipitate strokes.

Ginger, on the other hand, has none of these side effects. Ironically it has actually been shown to be a valuable *treatment* for gastrointestinal conditions, as well as *lowering* the risk of heart attack or stroke.

❭ Antimicrobial Effects

The hydrochloric acid found in the stomach is a powerful defence against ingested pathogens and rapidly destroys almost all organisms that are taken in with food. *Helicobacter pylori*, however, is an unusually resilient bacterial species that thrives in the hostile, extremely acidic environment of the stomach. Once established, this bacteria causes a range of problems including indigestion, oesophagitis, gastritis, stomach and duodenal ulcers, and stomach cancer. Ginger has traditionally been used as a treatment for stomach ailments, and it has recently been shown to kill all nineteen pathogenic *Helicobacter pylori* species. The regular ingestion of ginger should help to kill these dangerous bacteria before they become established, and thereby pre-empt the need for antibiotics which destroy many valuable intestinal bacteria, in addition to their intended targets.

Garlic
Allium sativa

CHAPTER 20

Anticancer, cardioprotective, antidiabetic, anti-Alzheimer's disease, anti-obesity, immunomodulator, antimicrobial

Garlic, which is the bulb of a plant native to the Himalayas and Siberia, is among the world's most important spices – both from a culinary and a medical perspective. Used across the globe as a pungent food flavouring, in many societies garlic is employed as an important medicinal spice with an array of traditional uses. These include its use as an antiseptic, anti-asthmatic, antirheumatic and as a treatment for coughs and colds. Over the centuries, it has also been employed against specific disease scourges, notably leprosy, plague and smallpox.

Garlic is one of the most thoroughly studied of all the spices, and its age-old medicinal reputation has been shown to be well deserved. It is an invaluable source of numerous important phytochemicals and contains over 25 valuable antioxidants. It is also an effective therapeutic and preventive agent against several acute conditions as well as a range of our most serious chronic diseases.

Important Phytochemicals

Antioxidants: Allicin, alliin, allyl-mercaptan, apigenin, caffeic acid, chlorogenic acid, coumaric acid, diallyl-pentasulfide, diallyl-trisulfide, ferulic acid, glutathione, hydroxy benzoic acid, kaempferol, lignin, myricetin, oleanolic acid, phytic acid, quercetin, rutin, s-allyl-l-cysteine, s-allyl-cysteine-sulfoxide, salicylic acid, sinapic acid, taurine, vanillic acid

Others: Ajoene, arginine, cycloalliin, diallyl disulfide, diallyl sulphide, tryptophan

Medicinal Properties

▶ Cancer

The regular consumption of garlic has a protective effect against a number of different malignancies, including cancers of the colon, breast, bladder, liver, prostate, lung, and leukaemia. While not all the chemo-protective mechanisms through which garlic works are understood, it is known to suppress COX-2 activity which is associated with inflammation and malignancy. It also inhibits *Helicobacter pylori* infection of the stomach, preventing ulceration caused by this bacteria and thereby reducing the risk of stomach cancer.

Garlic's anti-tumourigenic properties are, in part, due to its protective effect against some harmful ingested toxins. Aflatoxin, for example, is a liver carcinogen derived from the *Aspergillus flavus* fungus that grows on poorly stored grains, groundnuts and other crops. This puts societies that have inadequate storage facilities particularly at risk of developing liver cancer. Two of garlic's principal compounds, *diallyl sulphide* and *diallyl disulfide*, render aflatoxin harmless by modulating its metabolism and accelerating its breakdown in the liver. It is highly probable that the allyl sulphides and other compounds found in garlic plants also protect us against a range of other carcinogenic substances.

▶ Cardiovascular Disease and Blood Lipids

Garlic has long been used as an alternative treatment for the conditions underlying cardiovascular disease, and numerous studies have shown that this remarkable spice reduces all the major risk factors for the disease. Garlic works through the following mechanisms:

☐ *Lowers blood lipids:* Garlic reduces both cholesterol and triglyceride levels thereby reducing the risk of atherosclerosis.

☐ *Reverses atherosclerosis:* Garlic has a direct effect on atherosclerosis by inhibiting and even reversing the deposition of cholesterol in the arterial endothelial layer.

☐ *Reduction of platelet stickiness:* By preventing the excessive aggregation of platelets, garlic can reduce the risk of both heart attacks and thrombotic strokes. This property has been attributed principally to the phytochemical, *ajoene.*

☐ *Lowers blood pressure:* Garlic stimulates the synthesis of nitric oxide which is an important chemical involved in the vascular dilatation mechanism. By increasing the levels of nitric oxide in the blood, garlic increases vasodilatation and thereby lowers blood pressure. Interestingly, reduced nitric oxide levels are also associated with erectile dysfunction, and drugs such as Viagra work by increasing nitric oxide levels. Thus garlic's reputation in folk lore as an aphrodisiac may be justified after all.

❱ Diabetes

Garlic has blood glucose-lowering properties and also has the ability to reduce the raised blood lipid levels that are commonly found in diabetic patients.

❱ Alzheimer's Disease

Little is understood about the processes involved in Alzheimer's disease, but one of the few pathological mechanisms known to be common to these patients is the formation of amyloid plaques in the brain. Promising laboratory studies show that garlic can reduce amyloid deposition by up to 30 percent, suggesting that, along with turmeric, it is an important spice to use in the prevention, and possibly the treatment of this disease.

❯ Obesity

Garlic has several properties which make it an important substance in the management of obesity and is a valuable component of any weight loss strategy. These properties include the following:

- ☐ *Reduction of fat absorption:* Garlic contains *ajoene* which is an inhibitor of lipase, a pancreatic enzyme that breaks down dietary fat. Inhibition of lipase by garlic interferes with the absorption of dietary fat and thereby reduces the calorific intake of high-fat meals.
- ☐ *Appetite control:* Leptin is a signalling hormone produced by fat cells that influences the appetite. However, some individuals do not respond normally to leptin, resulting in an insatiable appetite and obesity. By increasing the brain's sensitivity to leptin, garlic can assist such individuals to reduce their food intake.

❯ Immunomodulation

Many of garlic's preventive and therapeutic effects are, directly or indirectly, attributable to its immunomodulatory properties. For example, some garlic compounds stimulate the proliferation of several white blood cell lines and induce the infiltration of tumours by white blood cells such as natural killer cells and macrophages. They also stimulate the release of tumour necrosis factor, interferon and other cytokines that are crucial to the prevention and spread of cancer.

❯ Antimicrobial Effects

Garlic is one of the most potent antimicrobial spices. It is capable of killing a wide range of bacteria, fungi and viruses, and studies are presently being undertaken to investigate its effectiveness against some of our more dangerous viral diseases. These include hepatitis, HIV, and the opportunistic bacterial and fungal infections commonly seen in AIDS patients.

Notes on the Medicinal Use of Garlic

☐ *Garlic products:* There are several garlic preparations on the market that make a number health claims. Some of these products have been subjected to clinical trials and are probably as effective as the natural spice. However, while techniques such as aging the garlic extract may improve some of its properties, other phytochemicals are lost during these processes. Thus the final product may not provide the broad spectrum of protection offered by the unadulterated spice.

☐ *Dosage:* It is important to take garlic in moderation as there are reports of adverse effects when high quantities of this plant have been ingested. A sensible guideline is to take no more than the maximum amount that would be used in a recipe that calls for significant quantities of this spice. In the context of prevention, one or two cloves a day should be adequate.

☐ *Control of "unsociable" side effects:* The negative effects of garlic on breath can be overcome to a certain extent by ingesting garlic in small amounts on a regular basis rather than larger, single doses of this spice.

CHAPTER 21

Onion

Allium cepa

Originally from East Asia, the onion is today one of the most widely cultivated and used of all vegetables. In some regions, especially in India, it is virtually a staple food and is regularly used in quantities that far exceed those typically seen in Western cooking. Onions also appear in the pharmacopeias of many traditional medical systems, in which, among other uses, they are valued as antiseptics and treatments for colds and flu. Sharing many properties with their close relative, garlic, onions can also assist in the prevention of several chronic diseases.

Important Phytochemicals

Antioxidants: Allicin, alliin, caffeic acid, catechol, coumaric acid, diallyl trisulfide, ferulic acid, fumaric acid, glutathione, isoquercitrin, isorhamnetin, kaempferol, lutein, melatonin, oleanolic acid, protocatechuic acid, pyrocatechol, quercetin, rutin, salicylates, sinapic acid, spiraeoside, vanillic acid

Others: Benzyl isothiocyanate, cepene, diallyl sulphide

Medicinal Properties

▶ Cancer

While there has been relatively little research into their anticancer properties, early studies suggest that the regular consumption of onions can significantly lower the incidence of lung cancer. The processes underlying this effect are not yet clear but may involve the phytochemical *quercetin,* a flavonol that is known to provide protection against a variety of cancer types.

▶ Cardiovascular Disease and Blood Lipids

Like garlic, onion's cardioprotective effects are multifaceted. Acting against each of the major risk factors for cardiovascular disease, onions lower cholesterol and high blood pressure, and reduce platelet stickiness.

▶ Diabetes

When administered in high doses, onion extracts can match the effectiveness of some of the modern antidiabetic drugs in the control of mild diabetes. This suggests that in normal culinary quantities onions can help prevent the onset of this disease.

▶ Osteoporosis

Onions stimulate a rise in bone mineral content and have been shown to increase bone thickness by up to 15 percent. A loss of bone density is often associated with a fall in oestrogen and deficiency of this hormone is a major causative factor of osteoporosis in women. Interestingly, even in the presence of low levels of oestrogen, onions continue to be effective and can reduce bone loss by up to 25 percent.

Fenugreek

Trigonella foenum graecum

> *Cardioprotective, blood lipid modulator, antidiabetic, hormone modulator, endurance enhancer*

The seeds of fenugreek are the most valuable part of the plant and have long been used as a nourishing dietary spice in its native Middle East, India and the Far East. It is also an important constituent of curries. In traditional medicine, fenugreek has been used to treat a number of conditions including diabetes, sore throats, and in poultices used to treat sores and abscesses. Recent investigations into the medicinal properties of this spice suggest it is important not only as a preventive for chronic diseases such as diabetes, but also for enhancing normal physiological processes, especially with respect to athletic performance.

Important Phytochemicals

Antioxidants: Apigenin, coumaric acid, genistein, isoorientin, isoquercitrin, isovitexin, kaempferol, lignin, luteolin, orientin, phytic acid, quercetin, quercitrin, rutin, selenium, superoxide-dismutase, vitexin

Others: Diosgenin, fenugreekine, trigonelline

Medicinal Properties

▶ Cardiovascular Disease and Blood Lipids

Fenugreek has a strong modulating effect on blood lipid levels and can substantially reduce the risk of atherosclerosis. In diabetics, who usually suffer lipid imbalances, it has demonstrated a remarkable ability to lower cholesterol, triglycerides and LDL levels while raising HDL levels. Another property of fenugreek is the reduction of platelet aggregation which, in turn, dramatically reduces the risk of abnormal blood clotting associated with heart attacks and strokes. Like most spices, fenugreek also contains many important antioxidants and has the added benefit of protecting other dietary and internally produced antioxidants from free-radical damage. This has important cardioprotective benefits, as well as helping to fortify the body against a range of other chronic conditions.

▶ Diabetes

Fenugreek, which has comparable antidiabetic potency to cinnamon, is one of the most valuable spices for the control of glucose metabolism and thus the prevention and treatment of Type II diabetes. Working in a similar way to the common antidiabetic drug glibenclamide, fenugreek lowers cellular insulin resistance and controls blood glucose homeostasis. It has been shown to lower blood glucose levels of Type II diabetics by as much as 46 percent. It also increases the levels of several important antioxidants and reduces the damaging oxidation of lipids associated with diabetes. As an added bonus, fenugreek seeds are very rich in a type of dietary fibre that modulates post-prandial blood glucose levels by delaying the absorption of sugar in the intestines.

Fenugreek is also effective against diabetes-related cataracts which occur commonly in diabetics. The enzymes that control glucose uptake into the lens of the eye do not function normally in diabetics and, as a result, glucose and its metabolites, fructose and sorbitol, accumulate in the lens tissues. The lenses of diabetic patients are also prone to damage by enzymes that would normally protect against destructive free radicals, and a combination of these factors leads to the gradual opacification of the lens known as a cataract. As fenugreek has been shown to partially reverse both the metabolic changes in the lens and to reduce the density of the cataract, it is likely to be even more effective as a prophylactic agent against cataract formation in diabetics.

❱ Endurance

One of the greatest difficulties facing athletes who compete in endurance events is maintaining a readily available supply of energy in the body. In order to achieve this, muscle carbohydrate stores, in the form of glycogen, must be continuously replenished. In an event lasting more than one-and-a-half hours, glycogen stores become depleted, and for the remainder of the event the athlete has to rely on external sources of energy, such as high carbohydrate drinks, which are inferior to glycogen as an energy source. Post-event re-synthesis of glycogen is also very important, and the two hours immediately following prolonged exercise is the crucial time for this process to occur.

Fenugreek has been shown to have a strong effect on glycogen replenishment; increasing post-event re-synthesis by over 60 percent in some endurance athletes. While its effects on glycogen re-synthesis during an event have yet to be tested, fenugreek is likely to exhibit a similarly beneficial effect during, as well as after, exercise.

❱ Hormones

Fenugreek is one of the richest sources of phytoestrogens and is thus a very useful spice for women who have low oestrogen levels. Phytoestrogens are also thought to help protect against certain types of cancer, and fenugreek may well be proven to have anti-tumourigenic effects should this property be investigated in the future.

❱ Nutrients

Fenugreek is one of the richest sources of selenium, which is among the most important antioxidant micronutrients. When consumed regularly, selenium appears to have a protective effect against a range of cancers, including those of the colon, lung and prostate. Recent evidence also shows that selenium helps to prevent the progression of HIV and other chronic viral illnesses.

Green tea
Camellia sinensis

Anticancer, cardioprotective, anti-obesity, anti-inflammatory, protects against toxins

Green tea and black tea are derived from the same plant, but they are processed in different ways. Green tea is prepared by allowing the leaves to dry fairly rapidly before they are packaged. The processing of black tea takes longer and involves a fermentation process that alters both the flavour and chemistry of the product. While many of the original phytochemicals found in the fresh leaves, such as caffeine, remain the same in both teas, some important compounds found in green tea are destroyed by fermentation and thus do not occur in black tea.

In many Eastern countries, green tea is the beverage of choice and the health benefits associated with its regular consumption in Eastern societies have been well documented. A number of laboratory studies have substantiated green tea's medicinal properties, which are believed to be primarily due to *epigallocatechin gallate* and other valuable catechin compounds that are destroyed by fermentation. Thus although black tea has some preventive properties, the absence of catechins and of other antioxidants lost during fermentation means that green tea is by far the superior medicinal beverage. We can all benefit from regularly consuming green tea and for those unable to tolerate caffeine, decaffeinated green tea is now widely available.

Important Phytochemicals

Antioxidants: Apigenin, catechin, caffeic acid, caffeine, carvacrol, chlorogenic acid, cinnamic acid, epicatechins, epigallocatechin gallate, eugenol, kaempferol, lycopene, myricetin, naringenin, polyphenols, quercetin, quercitrin, rutin, salicylates, tannic acid, thymol, vitexin, zeaxanthin

Others: Astragalin, farnesol, gallic acid, geraniol

Medicinal Properties

▶ Cancer

Green tea is one of the most valuable of all the anti-tumourigenic plants, and its cancer-preventing effects are undoubtedly its most important health benefit. Not only are the anticancer properties of green tea very powerful, but they are not specific to one cancer type; epidemiological and clinical evidence points to its preventive effects against cancer of the breast, prostate, lung, and some types of leukaemia.

Most of the research to date has focused on the antioxidant *epigallocatechin gallate* (EGCG) that, until recently, has been given most of the credit for green tea's cancer-preventing effects. However, as is so often the case, it is becoming clear that a number of other compounds are also responsible for these health benefits. Some of the newer studies have shown that, in fact, the caffeine found in green tea has anti-tumourigenic effects too.

EGCG and other phytochemicals found in tea are known to exert their anti-cancer properties via the following mechanisms:

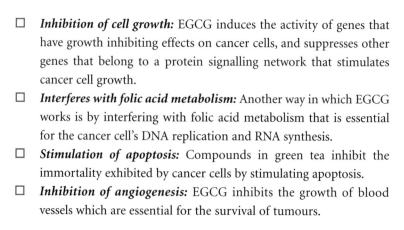

- ☐ *Inhibition of cell growth:* EGCG induces the activity of genes that have growth inhibiting effects on cancer cells, and suppresses other genes that belong to a protein signalling network that stimulates cancer cell growth.
- ☐ *Interferes with folic acid metabolism:* Another way in which EGCG works is by interfering with folic acid metabolism that is essential for the cancer cell's DNA replication and RNA synthesis.
- ☐ *Stimulation of apoptosis:* Compounds in green tea inhibit the immortality exhibited by cancer cells by stimulating apoptosis.
- ☐ *Inhibition of angiogenesis:* EGCG inhibits the growth of blood vessels which are essential for the survival of tumours.

▶ Cardiovascular Disease and Blood Lipids

Green tea has a dual cardioprotective effect. It reduces the risk of heart disease and strokes both indirectly, by lowering blood lipids, and directly, by inhibiting the deposition of cholesterol in the arterial walls.

▶ Obesity

Green tea can help overweight individuals lose weight, and its regular consumption is a valuable means to help treat and prevent of obesity. Interestingly, while green tea increases the loss of fat mass, it has no adverse effect on muscle mass.

Green tea's anti-obesity properties have been attributed primarily to EGCG, which works through the following complementary mechanisms:

- ☐ *Appetite reduction:* EGCG reduces the appetite by down-regulating the appetite stimulating hormone leptin.
- ☐ *Reduces fat absorption:* It interferes with the absorption of fat from the intestines, reducing the amount of calories that are ingested during a meal.
- ☐ *Inhibits fat storage:* By antagonising the conversion of glucose into fat, EGCG can reduce the amount of excess energy that is converted into fat. EGCG also promotes the uptake of glucose into muscle cells where it is stored as the carbohydrate, glycogen.
- ☐ *Increases metabolic rate:* EGCG and caffeine act synergistically on the nervous system to increase the metabolic rate which, in turn, increases fat "burn off" thereby assisting in weight loss.

▶ Arthritis

The antioxidants in green tea have been shown to check the over-production of several pro-inflammatory cytokines that are responsible for inflammation of the joints and other tissues associated with arthritis.

❱ Protection Against Toxins

The phytochemicals in green tea defend the body, in particular DNA, against toxins in two principal ways. They act directly, by protecting cellular DNA against free radical oxidants and other potent toxins, including arsenic. They also work by enhancing the detoxification enzymes superoxide dismutase and catalase, two internally produced antioxidants that play an important role in toxin neutralization. Green tea's protective effects against toxins thus contribute to its anticancer and other disease-preventing properties.

Grape
Vitis vinifera

CHAPTER 24

Anticancer, cardioprotective, anti-Alzheimer's disease

Although grapes are not generally thought of as spices, both wine and grape vinegar are used in condiments and to flavour a wide range of dishes.

The potent medicinal properties of grapes and grape products have been attributed to a variety of phytochemicals, and in particular to *resveratrol*. It is this compound that is thought to be largely responsible for the remarkable health-enhancing and disease-preventing properties of red wine. Importantly, this means that it is not essential to consume red wine in order to obtain the medicinal effects of resveratrol or other beneficial substances that occur in grapes. Red grape juice or red wine vinegar are valuable alternative sources of resveratrol and other phytochemicals, and when consumed regularly can offer similar protective benefits to those provided by red wine.

Important Phytochemicals

Antioxidants: Caffeic acid, chlorogenic acid, delphinidin, ellagic acid, epicatechin, gallic acid, lutein, luteolin, lycopene, malic acid, myricetin, proanthocyanidins, quercetin, resveratrol, rutin, salicylates

Others: Alpha-linolenic acid, beta ionone, betaine, biotin, cinnamic acid, coumarin, ferulic acid, geraniol, limonene

Medicinal Properties

▶ Cancer

Resveratrol has been shown to have both preventive and therapeutic effects against certain skin tumours. It does this via two mechanisms: by inhibiting the action of the pro-tumour protein *survivin*, and by up-regulating a protein that enhances apoptosis in skin cancer cells. Grapes are also a good source of the important antioxidant, *lycopene*, which has strong preventive properties against several malignancies, especially cancer of the prostate.

It is highly likely that grapes' anti-tumourigenic benefits will eventually be shown to extend to a wide range of cancers. Already, ongoing research into several other grape-derived compounds is pointing to its prophylactic effects against a number of different cancer types.

▶ Cardiovascular Disease and Blood Lipids

The cardioprotective benefits of grapes are affected by several different mechanisms. *Resveratrol, catechin* and *quercetin* all have valuable cholesterol-lowering properties. Resveratrol also directly retards the deposition of cholesterol plaques in the coronary and other arteries by inhibiting the oxidation of blood lipids. This anti-atherogenic property is complemented by resveratrol's stimulating effect on the enzymes that enhance the production of nitric oxide. A powerful blood vessel dilator, nitric oxide is vital to the control of high blood pressure and thereby to the prevention of heart attacks.

▶ Alzheimer's Disease

Grape-derived polyphenols show promising effects against Alzheimer's disease, as early studies suggest that they can both inhibit the deposition of amyloid in the brain as well as enhance the de-aggregation of existing amyloid plaques.

Rosemary
Rosmarinus officinalis

CHAPTER 25

Anticancer, cardioprotective, anti-Alzheimer's disease, antitoxin, anti-allergy

The leaves of this hardy Mediterranean plant are used to flavour a variety of dishes and beverages, and are added to some cosmetics. In its long and colourful history, rosemary has been used, among other things, as a symbol of fidelity and a guard against evil spirits and bad dreams. It has also gained an important place in traditional medicine, including its use as an antiseptic and as a treatment for respiratory problems, stomach cramps and arthritic pain. Rosemary is also believed to enhance the memory. More recently, it has become clear that rosemary is a valuable preventive agent against several chronic diseases and is one of several spices that contribute to the health-promoting effects of the "Mediterranean" diet.

Important Phytochemicals

Antioxidants: Apigenin, borneol, caffeic acid, carvacrol, chlorogenic acid, hesperidin, myrcene, oleanolic acid, rosmarinic acid, salicylates, ursolic acid

Others: Borneol, bornyl acetate, carnosol, cineole, camphor, geraniol, limonene, luteolin, pinenes, safrole, terpinenes

Medicinal Properties

▶ **Cancer**

Rosemary contains significant quantities of several antioxidants which exhibit potent anti-tumourigenic properties. These include *apigenin, salicylates, caffeic acid* and *ursolic acid*.

❱ Cardiovascular Disease and Blood Lipids

Like oregano, rosemary has cardioprotective, antioxidant and anti-inflammatory effects, and two of its compounds, *carvacrol* and *rosmarinic acid*, directly prevent the formation of atheromatous plaques in the arteries. *Oleanolic* and *ursolic acid* reduce the risk of atherogenesis even further by lowering abnormal blood lipid levels, while *caffeic acid* prevents platelet aggregation.

❱ Alzheimer's Disease

Rosmarinic acid has shown promising preventive and, in some cases, therapeutic effects against Alzheimer's disease. Although its mechanisms are not fully understood, like the phytochemicals in garlic and turmeric, rosmarinic acid prevents the deposition of amyloid plaque in the brain and may also contribute to its breakdown.

❱ Toxins

Rosemary has specifically been shown to protect the liver from damage by environmental toxins. More broadly, potent antioxidants present in rosemary, such as *rosmarinic acid* and *caffeic acid*, are effective scavengers of free-radical toxins and assist in the prevention of inflammatory diseases, cardiovascular disease and cancer.

❱ Allergies

The traditional use of rosemary as a treatment for respiratory problems has now been validated by clinical studies investigating its anti-allergenic properties. These have demonstrated that rosemary is an effective therapy for hay fever and asthma-causing allergies, and these anti-allergenic properties may well extend to other types of allergies.

Oregano
Origanum vulgare

CHAPTER 26

Anticancer, cardioprotective, anti-inflammatory

Oregano, that is today most strongly associated with the distinctive taste of pizza, has for centuries been used to flavour a variety of fish, meats and vegetable dishes in the Mediterranean region. Oregano also has a long history of medicinal uses, including the treatment of respiratory ailments, arthritis, wounds and indigestion. While there have been relatively few scientific investigations into its medicinal properties, oregano is a source of many potent phytochemicals that are known to be active against a range of pathological processes and chronic diseases.

Important Phytochemicals

Antioxidants: Caffeic acid, carvacrol, eugenol, hydroquinone, myrcene, oleanolic acid, phenol, phytosterols, rosmarinic acid, terpinenes, ursolic acid

Others: Carvone, caryophyllene, citral, geraniol, limonene, pinenes

Medicinal Properties

❱ Cancer

Oregano's anti-tumourigenic phytochemicals are both numerous and efficacious against a variety of cancer types. They include the anti-oxidants, *caffeic acid, eugenol, myrcene, oleanolic acid* and *ursolic acid*, as well as the non-antioxidant compounds, *carvone, caryophyllene, geraniol* and *limonene*.

❯ Cardiovascular Disease and Blood Lipids

In addition to possessing cardioprotective, antioxidant and anti-inflammatory properties, oregano contains *carvacrol* and *rosmarinic acid* which specifically inhibit the formation of atheromatous plaques. *Oleanolic* and *ursolic acid*, meanwhile, are effective at lowering abnormal blood lipid levels, while *caffeic acid* reduces platelet stickiness, and *eugenol* prevents the abnormal thrombus formation associated with heart attacks.

❯ Anti-inflammatory Effects

Oregano contains significant quantities of a number of well-known anti-inflammatory compounds and is likely to have protective effects against the many chronic diseases that are associated with underlying inflammatory processes. These anti-inflammatory compounds include *caffeic acid, carvacrol, eugenol, rosmarinic acid* and *ursolic acid*.

Thyme
Thymus vulgaris

CHAPTER **27**

Anticancer, cardioprotective, anti-inflammatory

The leaves of thyme lend a distinctive flavour to a variety of Mediterranean and French dishes. Used by the ancient Egyptians for embalming, thyme has, in addition to its culinary uses, been burnt as incense, given to warriors to instill courage and taken to enhance mental function. In traditional medicine, thyme is valued as an antiseptic and has also been used to treat sore throats, arthritis, colic and fevers. It also has cardioprotective and cancer-preventing properties that make this spice an important contributor to the beneficial health consequences of eating a "Mediterranean" type diet.

Important Phytochemicals

Antioxidants: Apigenin, caffeic acid, chlorogenic acid, eugenol, ferulic acid, gallic acid, kaempferol, luteolin, myrcene, naringenin, oleanolic acid, rosmarinic acid, salicylates, thymol, ursolic acid, vanillic acid

Others: Alpha-linolenic acid, borneol, carvacrol, citrol, geraniol, limonene, pinenes, terpenes

Medicinal Properties

▶ Cancer

Many of the phytochemicals present in thyme, notably some of its antioxidants, have well established anti-tumourigenic properties against a variety of cancer types. The most important of these cancer-preventing compounds include *caffeic acid, eugenol, ferulic acid, kaempferol, limonene, naringenin* and the *salicylates.*

163

▶ Cardiovascular Disease and Blood Lipids

Thyme contains a number of cardioprotective chemicals. *Alpha-linolenic acid*, for example, helps to lower high blood pressure and reduces platelet stickiness, as do *caffeic acid, ferulic acid, kaempferol, naringenin* and *thymol*. *Eugenol* and *oleanolic acid* lower cholesterol, while *chlorogenic acid* and *rosmarinic acid* have been shown to inhibit the development of atherosclerosis.

▶ Anti-inflammatory Properties

At least half of the phytochemicals present in thyme, in particular *eugenol, ferulic acid, kaempferol* and the *salicylates*, are effective anti-inflammatory agents. Often acting synergistically, the phytochemicals in this one spice provide a valuable artillery against the numerous inflammatory processes that underlie so many of our chronic diseases.

Citrus Zest
Citrus species

CHAPTER 28

Anticancer, blood lipid lowering, antimicrobial

Citrus fruits, including oranges, lemons, limes, grapefruit, tangerines and mandarins, are some of the most numerous and widely consumed fruits in the world today. As well as being eaten as fruits and juices, citrus peels, which contain the greatest concentration of their valuable phyto-chemicals, are frequently used as "zest", seasonings that add flavour to a variety of preserves, and sweet and savoury dishes.

Until recently, the perceived medicinal properties of citrus have been associated primarily with vitamin C (ascorbic acid), which occurs in high concentrations in all of the citrus species. Oranges are considered the "gold standard" in terms of food vitamin C content and the use of limes by the British navy to prevent its sailors developing the vitamin C-deficiency disease, scurvy, is one of the most well-known historical uses of food in a medicinal context. However, as we learn more about plants and the chemicals they contain, it is becoming clear that many other phytochemicals found in citrus contribute towards the extensive health benefits that are often still attributed to vitamin C.

Important Phytochemicals

Antioxidants: Ascorbic acid, genistic acid, lycopene, naringenin, neohesperidin, rutin, tangeretin

Others: Auraptine, hesperetin, limonin, lutein, nobiletin, pectin, quercetin, zeaxanthin

165

Medicinal Properties

▶ Cancer

As anticancer agents, citrus fruits have been subject to considerable research and have been shown to work against a number of cancer types. The fibre in citrus, called pectin, has also been studied and found to reduce the progression of advanced prostate cancer. Pectin can also lower the risk of a recurrence of mouth and throat cancers. Citrus fruits prevent cancer through the mechanisms outlined below.

- ☐ *Antioxidants*: Antioxidants are also powerful antimutagens, protecting our DNA from cancer-causing damage, and citrus fruits contain high concentrations of flavonoid antioxidants as well as a number of other potent antioxidant compounds. *Lycopene*, in particular, which has been shown to protect against prostate and other cancers, is found in large quantities in citrus fruits.
- ☐ *DNA repair*: The antioxidant *naringenin* not only helps prevent DNA damage, but also enhances DNA repair thereby reducing the chances of cancer development.
- ☐ *Cancer cell death*: The phytochemical *nobilitin* destroys cancer cells in two ways. It acts as a cytotoxin, killing cancer cells directly, and it can also work indirectly, inducing apoptosis and interfering with the cell cycles involved in certain types of liver cancer. It has also been shown to be effective in preventing the onset of cancers of the colon, breast and some leukaemias. It also exhibits synergism with certain anticancer drugs and reduces the resistance that cancer cells develop to these conventional treatments.
- ☐ *Inhibition of tumour growth*: *Coumarins* exhibit antitumour properties as does *tangeretin*, which can inhibit the proliferation of tumours by interfering with the signalling mechanism between the tumour cells.

☐ *Toxin inhibition:* The phytochemicals *naringenin* and *quercetin* protect us against NNK which is one of the most potent inducers of lung cancer. NNK is a strong tobacco-related environmental carcinogen to which both smokers and non-smokers are exposed. These two compounds work by inhibiting the activity of liver enzymes that convert NNK into a carcinogenic metabolite.

▶ Cardiovascular Disease and Blood Lipids

The polyphenol flavonoids, especially those found in grapefruit, are effective in lowering abnormal cholesterol and triglyceride levels, as is citrus pectin which also contributes to the cardioprotective effects of the polyphenols. Citrus flavonoids are powerful antioxidants – even more so than vitamin E – and when taken in their natural form their effects are enhanced by the presence of high levels of vitamin C found in citrus. In this way citrus also helps to reduce the oxidation of LDL cholesterol which is associated with the development of atherosclerosis.

▶ Antimicrobial Properties

Grapefruit seed extract has been found to be effective against more than 800 bacterial and viral strains, 100 strains of fungi, and a large number of single and multi-celled parasites – even when the microbes are diluted several hundredfold, to the point where there is no toxicity to human cells. This suggests that when regularly ingested, these seeds can help our bodies ward off infections, even in their earliest stages.

Mustard
Brassica species

Anticancer, antioxidant, anti-toxin

This seed spice native to the Mediterranean region is derived from several varieties of mustard plant, each of which produces seeds of a different intensity and flavour. All mustard plants belong to the brassica family that also includes horseradish, wasabi, cabbage, Brussels sprouts, broccoli, rocket, garden cress and watercress.

In addition to being valued internationally as spices and foods, brassicas have a notable history of use in traditional medicines. Mustard, for example, has been used to relieve headaches, as an emetic, for colds and flu and to treat arthritis. More recently, interest in the brassicas' medicinal properties has focused on broccoli, Brussels sprouts and cabbage that have been shown to have tremendous anticancer properties. However, because the members of this plant family contain the same phytochemicals, such protective qualities are likely to be common to all of the brassica species.

Important Phytochemicals

Antioxidants: Benzoic acid, caffeic acid, kaempferol, quercetin, sinapic acid, vanillic acid

Others: Indole-3-carbinol, isothiocyanates (most importantly the isothiocyanate, sulphorane)

168

Medicinal Properties

▶ Cancer

Brassicas comprise one of the most important groups of cancer preventing plants, both in terms of their diversity and efficacy. Not only do they help to protect against a variety of malignancies, including cancer of the pancreas, prostate, breast, stomach and colon, but as little as two or three servings per month may be enough for their anticancer properties to take effect. The prophylactic properties of this plant family have been attributed principally to several compounds, the most important of which are *indole-3-carbinol* and the *isothiocyanate* group of chemicals.

Although not all mechanisms through which brassicas exhibit anticancer effects are understood, the indoles, isothiocyanates and other compounds common to this family work in the following ways:

☐ *Inhibition of cancer-promoting enzymes:* Brassica phytochemicals can inhibit both carcinogen-activating enzymes as well as NF-κB, the overproduction of which is associated with many cancers including that of the pancreas.

☐ *Induction of apoptosis:* Isothiocyanates induce apoptosis by stimulating the production of reactive oxygen molecules in cancer cells.

☐ *Inhibition of inter-cellular communications:* By interfering with cytokine communications between cancer cells, brassica phytochemicals can slow the progression and spread of tumours.

☐ *Detoxification of carcinogens:* Indoles and isothiocyanates help protect DNA by increasing the activity of the liver enzymes that are responsible for the detoxification of carcinogens.

☐ *Excretion of PhIP:* Brassicas can increase the excretion of the powerful meat carcinogen PhIP by as much as 130 percent. This carcinogen is thought to be responsible for the increased risk of colorectal, breast and prostate cancers, all of which have been linked to excessive meat consumption.

☐ *Protection against hydrogen-peroxide damage:* Hydrogen peroxide is a powerful oxidant that is used by some immune cells to kill invading micro-organisms. However, in excess, it can cause damage to DNA, that may lead to accelerated aging, cancer and other diseases. Brassicas have been shown to be very effective at protecting white blood cell DNA against the damaging effects of surplus hydrogen peroxide.

❭ Antioxidants

Brassicas exhibit antioxidant effects through both direct and indirect mechanisms. In addition to several antioxidant phytochemicals that mop up free radicals themselves, they contain compounds that enhance the activity of both ingested and internally produced antioxidants. Sulphorane, for example, although not an antioxidant itself is an effective inducer of internally produced enzymes that, in turn, enhance the activity of the crucial intracellular antioxidant, glutathione. Sulphorane also catalyzes the production of the powerful antioxidant bilirubin.

❭ Antimicrobial properties

Although the primary focus of research into the brassicas has been in relation to their anticancer properties, they have also been shown to possess strong antimicrobial properties against a variety of bacteria and fungi. Brassicas cooked or steeped with contaminated meat for only ten minutes significantly reduce the bacterial counts in the meat, and they are likely to exhibit similar effects against other food-borne pathogens.

Soy
Glycine max

CHAPTER **30**

Anticancer, cardioprotective, anti-osteoporotic, hormone modulating

Soy is one of the most widely planted crops on the planet and in many countries is an important staple food. In addition to its use as a human and animal food, soy is processed to make condiments in the form of soy sauce, tamari, miso and others. Not only is the soy bean an excellent source of nutrients, it also contains several unique phytochemicals, most importantly the isoflavones, that exhibit powerful disease-preventing and health-enhancing properties. Soy is included in this book because, in addition to its value as a staple food, it provides some of the most well-researched, health-promoting compounds of all plants.

Important Phytochemicals

Antioxidants: Caffeic acid, catechin, chlorogenic acid, daidzein, daizin, ferulic acid, gallic acid, genistein, gossypol, isoquercitrin, lupeol, p-coumaric acid, phytosterols, pyridoxine, salicylic acid, vanillic acid

Others: Adenine, adenosine, alpha-linolenic acid, coumestrol, pyridoxine

---

Medicinal Properties

▶ Cancer

Populations with higher than average soy consumption typically have lower incidences of cancers of the breast, uterus, prostate, and colon. This protective effect is not completely understood, but is thought to be primarily due to the presence of the soy isoflavones, *genistein* and *daidzein*. Both compounds belong to the phytoestrogen group of plant chemicals that, when consumed regularly by women, can substantially reduce their risk of developing breast cancer.

Genistein, which is probably the most important chemopreventive component of soy, inhibits cancer at several stages during its development. Although not all of these mechanisms are clear, genistein is known to be a potent inhibitor of an enzyme, tyrosine kinase, a property that accounts for its ability to attenuate the growth of some cancer cell lines. Both genistein and daidzen exhibit anticancer effects by altering cancer-cell growth factor activity and by inhibiting malignant cell proliferation, differentiation, and angiogenesis.

▶ Cardiovascular Disease and Blood Lipids

Soy has multifaceted cardioprotective effects and is one of the most important plants for reducing the risk of heart disease and thrombotic strokes. Its does this via the following mechanisms:

☐ *Lowers blood lipids:* Numerous studies have shown soy to be effective at lowering cholesterol. This property, which was previously attributed to the fibre in soy, now appears to be due primarily to a combination of soy isoflavones, proteins and oligosaccharide carbohydrates – the latter are sugars that are fermented in the colon and generate short chain fatty acids that, once absorbed, hinder cholesterol synthesis in the liver. Soy also reduces the levels of potentially dangerous triglycerides and LDLs in the blood.

☐ *Inhibits atherosclerosis:* Genistein prevents the development of atherosclerosis by inhibiting cell adhesion – an integral part of atheromatous plaque formation.

☐ *Prevents lipid oxidation:* Soy isoflavones have potent antioxidant effects, preventing the oxidation of lipid particles that would otherwise contribute to the progression of atherosclerosis.

☐ *Improvement of vascular responsiveness*: Genistein and daidzen have favourable effects on vascular function by improving the ability of stiff, atherosclerotic blood vessels to dilate in response to the oxygen requirements of heart muscle and other tissues.

❯ Alzheimer's Disease

Soy isoflavones have shown promising effects against Alzheimer's disease and, particularly in post-menopausal women, are likely to reduce the risk of developing the disease. The isoflavones appear to work by preventing the malfunctioning of *tau* proteins in the brain that are associated with Alzheimer's disease.

❯ Bone Density

Osteoporosis occurs when the metabolism of bone is disrupted, resulting in the loss of calcium and other minerals, and a reduction in bone density. This causes the bones to become brittle and easily fractured. Soy isoflavones can be effective both in the prevention and treatment of this debilitating disease. Their structural similarity to human oestrogen is thought to be responsible for this property.

While osteoporosis is primarily due to a lack of calcium in the bone, it is not necessarily the result of an inadequate intake of calcium. In fact, the mechanism controlling the deposition and resorption of calcium has little to do with the amount of calcium in the diet and is influenced by a range of factors, including the levels of certain hormones such as oestrogen. If oestrogen levels are too low, then calcium resorption from bone overtakes deposition, resulting in a gradual reduction of bone density and the onset of osteoporosis. Isoflavones are therefore especially valuable preventive and therapeutic agents in postmenopausal women who typically have lower oestrogen levels than younger women.

▶ Menopause

A diet high in soy products raises the genistein and daidzen concentration in the body by up to twenty times, and this is associated with a dramatic improvement in menopausal symptoms. Hot flashes can decrease by over 50 percent and vaginal dryness by over 60 percent when the amount of soy in the diet is increased. Importantly, soy carries none of the breast cancer risks associated with the synthetic oestrogens used in hormone replacement therapy.

Chilies and Red Peppers
Capsicum species

CHAPTER 31

Anticancer, antioxidants, metabolic rate stimulants, analgesics

The capsicums are "New World" spices that are represented by many diverse species and cultivars, including chilies (*Capsicum fructescens*), paprika (*Capsicum annum*) and red peppers. The quantities of the various phytochemicals found in capsicums vary considerably between the different cultivars. Chilies, for example, tend to have very high concentrations of capsaicin which is the phytochemical that gives plants of this genus their strong flavour and irritant effects. Paprika and sweet red peppers contain smaller quantities of capsaicin, but higher concentrations of another important phytochemical called capsiate. There has to date been relatively little research into the effects of capsicums on chronic diseases, but new research showing a positive effect on liver cancer is likely to prompt further investigation into their prophylactic effects.

Important Phytochemicals

Antioxidants: Caffeic acid, capsaicin, chlorogenic acid, coumaric acid, ferulic acid, hesperidin, lutein, myrcene, quercetin, rutin, salicylates, scopoletin

Others: Beta-carotene, capsiate, capsidol, limonene, zeaxanthin

Medicinal Properties

▶ Cancer

Capsaicin, the antioxidant phytochemical found in particularly high quantities in chilies, has important anti-tumourigenic properties, specifically as a powerful inducer of apoptosis in liver cancer cells.

❯ Obesity

Both *capsaicin* and *capsiate* raise the body's metabolic rate and increase the rate of fat "burn-off". Capsaicin has the additional benefit of suppressing the appetite through its direct effect on the brain's satiety centre and by stimulating the release of anorectic hormones, like cholecystokinin, by the intestines.

❯ Analgesic Effects

A considerable body of research has shown capsicums to be very effective in the treatment of acute and chronic pain – notably the pain associated with shingles and arthritis. With respect to this property, it is likely that *capsaicin* acts as a counter-irritant (when applied in the form of a cream) or a stimulant of the body's natural endorphin painkillers. There is also some evidence that chilies can help to control the symptoms of irritable bowel syndrome.

Coriander

Coriandrum sativum

CHAPTER 32

Anticancer, blood lipid modulator, antidiabetic, chelating agent

Coriander is indigenous to southern Europe, but it is used widely in Asiatic and South American cuisine as well as that of the Mediterranean region. Coriander leaves are used to garnish salads and the roots feature regularly in Thai cooking. However, the small fruits (often called seeds) are the most important part of the plant and are a crucial ingredient of curry powders. Coriander is also used in a range of savoury dishes, desserts and confectioneries, as well as in liqueurs and perfumes. The same is true from a medicinal perspective, as the fruits contain the highest concentrations of all the important phytochemicals that occur in this plant. While there is still limited understanding of the mechanisms through which coriander acts, initial research indicates that it is effective as both a treatment and preventive agent for several chronic diseases.

> ## Important Phytochemicals
>
> **Antioxidants:** Caffeic acid, camphene, chlorogenic acid, isoquercitrin, myrcene, quercetin, rutin, vanillic acid
>
> **Others:** Angelicin, apigenin, beta-sitosterol, borneol, camphor, cineole, cinnamic acid, geraniol, limonene, myristicin, terpinenes

Medicinal Properties

❱ Cancer

Coriander's anti-tumourigenic properties have been demonstrated in relation to colon cancer. It works by protecting against the damaging effects of lipid oxidation associated with this malignancy. It is highly probable that coriander also contributes to the low incidences of several other cancer types seen in the populations of Eastern nations that consume large quantities of this spice.

▶ Cardiovascular Disease and Blood Lipids

Coriander lowers cholesterol and triglyceride levels, helping to reduce the risk of atherosclerosis and thereby heart attack and stroke. It does this through two mechanisms: by inhibiting the uptake of these lipids in the intestines, and by enhancing their breakdown and excretion.

▶ Diabetes

Coriander has dual blood glucose-lowering effects. It works both by enhancing the secretion of insulin from the pancreas and exhibiting insulin-like activity at cellular level.

▶ Chelation

Coriander is a powerful chelator of toxic heavy metals. It has been shown specifically to eliminate lead deposits from the kidneys and bones.

Cumin
Cuminum cyminum

CHAPTER 33

Anticancer, antioxidant, anti-inflammatory

This seed-derived spice native to the eastern Mediterranean has a millennia-long and diverse history of use by humans. In ancient Egypt, cumin was added to food as a condiment and used in the mummification of the dead. The Romans and ancient Greeks likewise used cumin in cooking and also for cosmetic purposes, and it is mentioned in the Bible as a form of payment. Today cumin is an important component of a variety of cuisines, including Middle Eastern, Indian, North African and South American. From a traditional medical perspective, cumin has been used both as an analgesic and to treat indigestion.

Although the scientific research into the medicinal properties of this spice is limited, cumin contains a number of effective antioxidants, some of which have been well researched, and early studies show promising anticancer and anti-inflammatory characteristics.

Important Phytochemicals

Antioxidants: Eugenol, gamma-terpinene, luteolin, myrcene, terpinolene

Others: Bornyl-acetate, carophyllene, carveol, cineole, dipentene, farnesol, limonene, pinenes, terpenes

Medicinal Properties

▶ Cancer and Antioxidant Effects

Cumin has been shown to have strong anti-tumourigenic properties and, although the mechanisms underlying this effect are not yet clear, they are in all likelihood due to the presence of the antioxidants and other

179

anticancer compounds, such as *limonene*, that occur in this spice. In addition to their direct antioxidant action, some of the compounds found in cumin have been shown to act synergistically to enhance the activities of two of the body's own antioxidants, superoxide dismutase and catalase.

▶ Anti-inflammatory Properties

Cumin's traditional use as a pain killer has been borne out by contemporary research that has shown it to be very effective in treating painful inflammatory conditions. It works as an anti-inflammatory analgesic not only when taken orally but gives relief when applied topically over painful, inflamed tissue.

Liquorice
Glycyrrhiza glabra

CHAPTER **34**

Anticancer, anti-inflammatory, immunomodulator, antimicrobial

Liquorice is a spice derived from the roots of a plant that originated in China. It has been used for thousands of years as a food additive and as a medicine, the latter as a treatment for sore throats, bronchitis, gastritis, constipation and other conditions. Today liquorice is used extensively to flavour confectionery, sweets, alcoholic drinks, beverages and various dishes in both the East and the West. It is also a constituent of many cough syrups and throat lozenges. Promising new research suggests that liquorice is an effective agent against several pathological mechanisms and chronic diseases.

Important Phytochemicals

Antioxidants: Apigenin, carvacrol, eugenol, ferulic acid, genistein, glycyrrhetic acid, glycyrrhetinic acid, glycyrrhizin, isoquercitrin, kaempferol, lignin, lupeol, maltol, mannitol, naringenin, phenol, quercetin, salicylic acid, sinapic acid, saponins, thymol, umbelliferone

Others: Glycrrhetinic acid, glycyrrhisoflavanone, glycrrhizan, isoflavones, licoflavones, licoricin, liquiritone

---

Medicinal Properties

❯ Cancer

Liquorice contains many phytochemicals, including *apigenin, eugenol, ferulic acid, genistein* and *naringenin* that have proven anticarcinogenic effects. Several of liquorice's phytochemicals also show strong anti-

181

microbial activities that help to protect individuals infected with hepatitis B and C viruses from developing liver cancer.

▶ Anti-inflammatory Effects

Liquorice contains several important anti-inflammatory phytochemicals that appear to work through two principal mechanisms. They can directly inhibit an abnormal inflammatory response as well as enhance the anti-inflammatory potency of some steroids.

▶ Immunomodulator

Glycerhizin is the major active phytochemical found in liquorice and works both as an immunomodulator and as a potent antiviral agent. It has even been shown to be effective against HIV, protecting the immune systems of HIV-infected individuals as well as lowering their viral loads.

▶ Stomach Ulcers

The long-standing use of liquorice as a treatment for stomach ulcers and gastritis has been confirmed by recent studies which found that the activity of the ulcer-causing bacteria, *Helicobacter pylori*, is inhibited by several phytochemicals found in this spice.

Caraway
Carum carvi

Caraway, which is believed to have been used for longer than any other European spice, is derived from the seeds of a biennial plant native to Europe and Asia. It is used in a variety of confectioneries, and is frequently added to cream cheese, breads and meat dishes. Infusions of caraway have traditionally been used as a digestive aid, and to relieve stomach pain, menstrual cramps, sore throats and coughs.

Important Phytochemicals

Antioxidants: Caffeic acid, camphene, carvacrol, coumaric acid, gamma terpinene, hyperoside, isoquercitrin, kaempferol, myrcene, myristicin, quercetin, scopoletin

Others: Carveol, carvone, limonene

Medicinal Properties

▶ Cancer

Caraway contains high levels of phytochemicals which reduce the activity, by up to ten times, of a class of enzymes that convert food-derived molecules and other ingested compounds into carcinogenic toxins. The potentially destructive molecules may originate from a variety of sources, including food contamination by agricultural and food-processing chemicals or atmospheric pollutants. Suppression of these enzymes helps to prevent a variety of cancers. In addition, other compounds found in caraway have been found to specifically inhibit the proliferation of liver cancer cells.

Caraway seeds are also one of the richest sources of *limonene*, a phytochemical common to several spices that inhibits the initiation of cancers of the lung, breast, stomach and liver by inducing apoptosis in malignant cells. The potency of limonene may increase dramatically in the presence of other synergistic phytochemicals, confirming the benefits of ingesting spices in their whole form, and preferably with other spices.

▶ Diabetes

Caraway is effective in lowering abnormally high glucose levels in diabetics. Raised glucose levels may be normalised after only two weeks after starting treatment with this spice, but it does not appear to affect normal blood glucose levels.

▶ Hormone Imbalances

Caraway seeds are a rich source of phytoestrogens and are a useful addition to the diets of women who have low estrogen levels. Caraway can thus be helpful in easing menopausal symptoms.

Caper

Capparis spinosa

CHAPTER 36

Blood lipid modulator, antidiabetic

Capers are the flower buds of a shrub native to the Mediterranean and Middle East and are usually pickled before being eaten or used as condiments. The most important phytochemicals present in capers are isothiocyanates, which are similar to those found in other spices of the brassica family: mustard, horseradish and wasabi. The isothiocyanates in brassicas have been found to have strong anticancer properties and, although the use of capers in preventing cancer has yet to be investigated, this spice is likely to exhibit similar effects. Contemporary research into the healing properties of capers has, however, focused principally on its use as a lipid-lowering and antidiabetic agent.

Important Phytochemicals

Antioxidants: Beta-sitosterol, beta-sitosterol-glucoside, quercetin, rutin, vitamin E

Others: Coumarin, glucosinolates, isothiocyanates

Medicinal Properties

▶ Cardiovascular Disease and Blood Lipids

Capers have shown strong blood lipid-lowering activity in individuals with abnormally high lipid levels. Only four days after beginning a regular dose of capers, blood cholesterol and triglyceride levels start to fall. After two weeks of this treatment, they have dropped considerably and often reach normal levels in some individuals.

185

❱ Diabetes

Abnormally high glucose levels in diabetics begin to fall after only one day of taking a caper extract, and after two weeks most patients have normal blood glucose levels. The exact mechanism of caper's glucose-lowering effect has not yet been established, but insulin levels stayed the same for the duration of the studies so their action is unlikely to be due to the stimulation of insulin release from the pancreas. As is the case with so many of the other antidiabetic spices, capers probably work by increasing the sensitivity of the cells' insulin receptors or by mimicking the effect of insulin on the receptors themselves. Interestingly, capers do not affect the blood sugar levels of non-diabetics.

Bay leaf
Laurus nobilis

CHAPTER 37

Anticancer, cardioprotective, anti-inflammatory

The leaves from the bay tree are used to flavour meats, poultry, seafood and many other dishes. The essential oil derived from bay is also used in the perfume and confectionery industries. In some societies, bay has symbolic importance and in the ancient Olympic Games the winner of each event was crowned with a garland of bay (laurel) leaves.

Important Phytochemicals

Antioxidants: Caffeic acid, camphene, carvacrol, catechins, coumaric acid, cyanidine, eugenol, kaempferol, mannitol, myrcene, proanthocyanidins, quercetin, rutin, salicylates, terpinenes, thymol

Others: Cineole, geraniol, linalool, limonene, parthenolide

Medicinal Properties

▶ Cancer

Bay leaf contains *caffeic acid*, *quercetin*, *eugenol* and *catechins*, all of which have chemoprotective properties against several different types of cancer. Another phytochemical found in bay, *parthenolide*, has been shown to specifically inhibit the proliferation of cervical cancer cells by inducing apoptosis, inhibiting tumour-associated angiogenesis and reducing the activity of the tumour promoter, NF-κB.

187

▶ Cardiovascular Disease

Bay leaf, which is an important component of Mediterranean seasonings, contains valuable compounds that contribute to the cardiovascular health benefits associated with the Mediterranean diet. The phyto-chemicals *caffeic acid*, *rutin*, and *salicylates* all have cardioprotective effects that contribute to a reduced risk of heart attack and stroke.

▶ Inflammation

Bay leaf has traditionally been used as a treatment for arthritis and other inflammatory conditions. This ancient knowledge about the plant has now been borne out by studies showing that *parthenolide*, which is contained in bay, is a COX-2 inhibitor and thereby an effective anti-inflammatory agent.

Other Spices

Although the spices in this chapter have not, as yet, attracted much research into their medicinal properties, they are rich in valuable antioxidants and other phytochemicals that have been shown to have preventive and therapeutic effects when researched in the context of other plants. In future, given the exemplary track record of many phytochemicals found in other spices, further studies will no doubt also reveal a variety of protective and therapeutic properties in the compounds present in these under-researched spices.

Allspice (Pimento)
Pimenta dioica

General notes	Phytochemicals	Medicinal Properties
Allspice is a "New World" spice that comes from the unripe fruit of a tree indigenous to the West Indies and Central America. The name allspice relates to its strong aroma which suggests a combination of cinnamon, clove, nutmeg and pepper.	*Antioxidants:* Eugenol, methyleugenol, myrcene, proanthocyanidins, quercetin, salicylates, terpenes *Others:* Chavicol, cinnamaldehyde, limonene	Among the spices, allspice has one of the highest concentrations of important antioxidants like proanthocyanidins that help protect against a range of diseases, including cardiovascular disease, cancer and neuro-degenerative conditions.

Anise
Pimpinella anisum

General notes	Phytochemicals	Medicinal Properties
Anise is a Mediterranean spice that, in the West, is used mainly to flavour confectionery. In its native countries, it is an important flavouring for alcoholic drinks like raki, ouzo and pernod. Traditionally it is used to treat coughs.	*Antioxidants:* Caffeic acid, camphene, chlorogenic acid, eugenol, myristicin, rutin *Others:* Bergapten, limonene, pinenes, terpinols	Anise contains limonene which is known to have an inhibitory effect against a number of cancers and eugenol which inhibits platelet aggregation.

Basil
Ocimum basilicum

General notes	Phytochemicals	Medicinal Properties
The leaves of the basil (or sweet basil) plant are used extensively as a condiment in both Eastern and Western cuisine. This spice's traditional non-culinary uses include as a digestive aid and an antiseptic. A number of basil's phyto-chemicals have been well researched in other spices and are known to have important medicinal properties.	*Antioxidants:* Apigenin, carophyllene, eugenol, geraniol, methyl eugenol, ursolic acid *Others:* Cineol, citral, linalool, methyl chavicol, methyl cinnamate	Basil contains several potent anti microbial chemicals. Ursolic acid and apigenin demonstrate strong activity against the herpes viruses, and apigenin is also effective against hepatitis viruses. Linalool helps fight adenoviruses that are responsible for the common cold and other respiratory infections like croup. The antioxidant eugenol inhibits platelet aggregation.

Cardamon
Elettaria cardamomum

General notes	Phytochemicals	Medicinal Properties
Cardamon is one of the most important spices in many Eastern cuisines and is used in some Middle Eastern countries for flavouring coffee. It is also a renowned breath freshen-er. As one of the most expensive of the spices, car-damon is exceeded in price only by saffron and vanilla.	*Antioxidants:* Caffeic acid, camphene, cyanidin, gamma-terpinene, gamma-tocopherol, salicylates *Others:* Camphor, cineole, cymene, linalool, palmitic acid, stearic acid, terpinene, vanillic acid	Cardamon contains several important antioxidants, notably the anti-inflammatory and cardioprotective salicylates. Like basil, cardamon also contains linalool which is an antiviral agent.

Clove *Syzygium aromaticum*		
General notes	Phytochemicals	Medicinal Properties
Cloves are the fruit of a tree indigenous to Indonesia. In addition to their culinary uses, cloves have mild analgesic properties and oil of clove has long been used in dentistry as a treatment for toothache.	*Antioxidants:* ß-caryophyllene, ellagic acid, eugenol, eugenol acetate, hyperoside, isoeugenol, isoquercitrin, kaempferol, methyl eugenol, myricetin, oleanolic acid, peduncula-gin, procyanidin, quercetin, rhamnetin *Others:* Eugenin, eugenyl acetate, syringic acid	Cloves are loaded with many highly effective antioxidants including procyanidin and quercetin. There is also evidence that eugenol and eugenol acetate inhibit platelet aggregation and thus protect against heart attack and thrombotic strokes.

Curry leaf *Murraya koenigii*		
General notes	Phytochemicals	Medicinal Properties
The curry leaf comes from a shrub native to India and is an important ingredient of spicy Eastern dishes. Ironically, it is seldom added to the "curry powders" used in the West, which generally consist of a combination of other spices such as cumin, coriander, black pepper, ginger and fenugreek.	*Antioxidants:* Carophyllene, carvacrol, mahanimbene, mahanine, myrcene *Others:* Limonene, linalool, pinenes	The curry leaf contains the antiviral compounds linalool and limonene, which have been shown to have protective effects against some cancers.

Dill
Anethum gravelans

General notes	Phytochemicals	Medicinal Properties
Dill seeds – and to a lesser extent the leaves of this plant – are used widely in European cuisines; to flavour eggs, meats, salads, confectioneries and pickles. Dill oil is used in some detergents and soaps. As a traditional medicine, dill is used to treat indigestion and infant colic.	*Antioxidants:* Anethole, beta-sitosterol, caffeic acid, carvacrol, chlorogenic acid, eugenol, ferulic acid, kaempferol myrcene, myristicin, quercetin, quercitrin, scopoletin *Others:* Alpha-linolenic acid, bergapten, carvone, esculetin, geraniol, glucoside, limonene, pinenes, terpineol, umbelliferone	Dill contains many valuable antioxidants, including eugenol which may inhibit platelet aggregation. It also contains limonene which exhibits preventive properties against some types of cancer.

Fennel
Foeniculum vulgare

General notes	Phytochemicals	Medicinal Properties
Fennel's strong-tasting seeds, which have a similar flavour to aniseed or liquorice, are used in many European dishes, to flavour fish, bread and confectionaries. The more subtly flavoured stalks are widely used as a vegetable and in salads. In ancient Greece fennel was known as 'marathon', because it grew at the famous battle site, and it was used as a symbol of victory.	*Antioxidants:* Caffeic acid, camphene, coumaric acid, ferulic acid, kaempferol, myrcene, myristicin, protocatechuic acid, quercetin, rutin, scopoletin, vanillic acid, vanillin *Others:* Bergapten, cineole, cinnamic acid, imperatorin, limonene, pinenes, psoralen, scoparone, terpinenes, trigonelline, umbelliferone	Fennel contains a variety of important antioxidants, including limonene, which has anticancer properties.

Marjoram *Origanum majorana*		
General notes	**Phytochemicals**	**Medicinal Properties**
Marjoram, native to Asia Minor and the Mediterranean, is closely related to oregano, both in its culinary uses and by way of its constituent phytochemicals. Its traditional medicinal applications include its use as a mild analgesic, an antiseptic and for the treatment of indigestion.	***Antioxidants:*** Apigenin, caffeic acid, carvacrol, catechol, chlorogenic acid, coumaric acid, eugenol, kaempferol, luteolin, myrcene, naringenin, oleanolic acid, protocatechuic acid, quercetin, rosmarinic acid, rutin, thymol, ursolic acid, vanillic acid, vitexin ***Others:*** Carvone, cineole, cinnamic acid, geraniol, pinenes, terpinenes	Like its relative, oregano, marjoram is packed with antioxidant phytochemicals, notably rosmarinic acid that inhibits the formation of atheromatous plaques and ursolic acid which can help to lower blood lipid levels. Marjoram also contains the same anticarcinogenic and anti-inflammatory chemicals as oregano.
Mints *Menthe species*		
General notes	**Phytochemicals**	**Medicinal Properties**
In addition to their important culinary uses, the mints, including peppermint and spearmint, are used in both traditional medical systems and in modern pharmaceuticals. Menthol, an ingredient in many medicines, is extracted from mint plants. The mints are also widely used as digestive aids in the form of teas.	***Antioxidants:*** Anethole, caffeic acid, carvacrol, chlorogenic acid, eugenol, hesperidin, luteolin, myrcene, p-coumaric acid, rosmarinic acid, rutin, thymol, vanillin ***Others:*** Cineole, coumarin, hesperidin, limonene, menthol, menthone, pinenes	Certain mints, especially peppermint, have some of the most potent antioxidant activities of all spices. These include rosmarinic acid, which inhibits atheromatous plaque formation in the arteries. Mints also contain limonene, that provides protection against some cancers.

Nutmeg (Mace)
Myrista fragrans

General notes	Phytochemicals	Medicinal Properties
Nutmeg is the seed, and mace the aril, of a tree native to Indonesia. Nutmeg is used to flavour confectionery as well as many savoury and sweet dishes. It also has some traditional medical uses, including as a treatment for diarrhoea. In high doses it has narcotic effects.	*Antioxidants:* Caffeic acid, camphene, coumaric acid, cyanidin, delphinidin, epicatechin, eugenol, isoeugenol, kaempferol, myrcene, myristicin, myristic acid, oleanolic acid, quercetin, terpinenes, vanillin *Others:* Elemicin, furfural, linalool, limonene, safrole	Nutmeg provides several important antioxidants, including eugenol which inhibits platelet aggregation and oleanolic acid which can lower blood lipids. It also contains limonene which has preventive properties against some cancers, and linalool which has anticancer and antiviral effects.

Parsley
Petroselinum crispum

General notes	Phytochemicals	Medicinal Properties
The leaves of this Mediterranean spice are commonly used as garnishes for salads and a variety of other dishes. The roots of certain varieties are also used as a vegetable. In traditional medicine, parsley has a number of uses, including the prevention of halitosis and the treatment of bladder and kidney problems.	*Antioxidants:* Apigenin, caffeic acid, caphene, chlorogenic acid, coumaric acid, kaempferol, myrcin, myristicin, naringenin, psoralen, quercetin, rosmarinic acid, rutin, terpenes *Others:* Bergapten, geraniol, imperatorin, limonene, lutein, psoralen, pinenes, xanthotoxin	Among many other potent antioxidants, parsley contains rosmarinic acid, that inhibits the formation of atheromatous plaques in arteries. It also contains the powerful anticancer compound, limonene.

194

Star Anise
Illicium verum

General notes	Phytochemicals	Medicinal Properties
Native to China, star anise is used to flavour confectionery and is a component of Chinese "five spice" powder. Among other medicinal uses, it is used as a treatment for arthritis and colic. It is also chewed to sweeten the breath.	*Antioxidants:* Anethole, camphene, hydroquinone, myrcene, proanthocyanidins, rutin, terpinene *Others:* Anisatin, anisaldehyde, cineole, limonene, linalool, trans-anethole	Among the spices, star anise is one of the most potent LDL cholesterol antioxidants and so plays a valuable role in preventing the development of atherosclerosis. It also contains limonene which has anticancer properties, and linalool which possesses both anticancer and antiviral activities.

Tarragon
Artemisia dracunculus

General notes	Phytochemicals	Medicinal Properties
Tarragon originates in Siberia and, although it is a fundamental component of the French *herbes de Provence*, it is not as widely used as many other European herbs. This is mainly because it loses much of its flavour when dried and is best used fresh. In traditional medicine, tarragon has been used to treat toothache, as a digestive aid and as a mild sedative.	*Antioxidants:* Anethole, apigenin, caffeic acid, chlorogenic acid, eugenol, ferulic acid, gallic acid, luteolin, myrcene, naringenin, quercetin, rosmarinic acid, rutin, salicylic acid *Others:* Cineole, coumarin, menthol	Tarragon contains an abundance of antioxidants, including the anti-inflammatory, salicylic acid, and other key phytochemicals that have well-established protective effects against cardiovascular disease, cancer and other degenerative conditions. It is one of the spices that contribute to the health of those eating a traditional "Mediterranean" type of diet.

CONCLUSION

Adding Spice to Your Life

CHAPTER 39

S U M M A R Y • S U M M A R Y • S U M M A R Y

☐ To ensure optimal health, phytochemicals should, like macronutrients, vitamins and minerals, be treated as essential dietary constituents – to be consumed on a daily basis.
☐ By fortifying our body's complex web of biochemical processes, phytochemicals work both individually and in concert to enhance health, slow the degenerative processes associated with aging and protect us against a multitude of serious chronic diseases.
☐ When consumed regularly, spices – which provide the richest and most diverse array of bioactive phytochemicals – provide an ideal means to obtain the maximum benefits from these remarkable substances.
☐ For those of us who have difficulty incorporating a sufficient diversity of spices into our diet, spice supplements offer a convenient way to ensure that our bodies are constantly awash with a variety of the most beneficial, potent and pharmacologically active phytochemicals.

▶ Fantastic Phytochemicals

Undoubtedly one of the most important outcomes of our ever expanding knowledge of diseases and their underlying biochemical processes is the realization that there is considerably more to the nutritional and medicinal value of food than was previously understood. It is beyond contention that macronutrients – in the form of carbohydrates, proteins and fats – cannot by themselves comprise a healthy diet. They must, at the very least, be augmented by a range of essential vitamin and mineral micronutrients. Moreover, it is becoming increasingly evident that, in addition to these, we need other essential compounds from our foods. An increasing and compelling body of evidence indicates that for optimal health we should ensure that our diets provide us with the widest possible assortment of the remarkable disease-preventing and health-enhancing phytochemicals found in common food plants.

The culinary spices and medicinal herbs that have been used in folk medicine to treat a wide range of diseases have also provided us with many drugs that are based on compounds extracted from these plants and which are now used to treat both acute and chronic diseases. Some of these phytochemicals have shown both preventive and therapeutic effects against some of our deadliest and most debilitating chronic diseases, including cancer, diabetes, heart disease and Alzheimer's disease. In many studies, they have been shown to be equally, if not more effective than modern drugs – and the plant-derived equivalents rarely have any of the unpleasant or dangerous side effects often associated with synthetic medicines. In addition to fortifying the body against disease, these remarkable compounds have adaptogenic characteristics. As such they are capable of enhancing normal, healthy biochemical processes and can, for example, improve post-event recovery in athletes.

Although these valuable compounds are present in a range of common foods, when measured by potency and variety, spices provide the most important source of medicinal phytochemicals. To date, most of the studies investigating the medicinal properties of spices and their constituent compounds have focused on their therapeutic attributes. It was, however, the prophylactic benefits of regular spice consumption that initially prompted much of the laboratory and clinical work. A number of fascinating epidemiological studies have pointed to the markedly lower incidences of chronic diseases that occur in populations that consume high quantities of spices. There is an increasing level of understanding of the pathological mechanisms that underlie the development, manifestation and progression of diseases, and the role that plant compounds play in interfering with these processes. This is tremendously exciting from a medical perspective; for while spice-derived phytochemicals may indeed provide valuable therapies for individual illnesses, prevention of disease is far cheaper and more effective than cure, and the greatest value of spices lies in their use as *preventive* agents.

❚ The Power of Prevention

The body's normal biochemical processes involve the interaction of thousands of chemicals, both internally synthesised molecules, as well as those derived from external sources. Underpinning health and physiological equilibrium is an intricate network of finely tuned biochemical processes that work to maintain normal homeostasis. This biochemical web can work adequately without a full complement of strands, but the more of these that it has the more resilient it will be, the longer it will last and the more effectively it will function in the face of pathogenic agents and degeneration. The disruption of one or more of these processes, if uncorrected, may eventually result in the onset of disease; helping to prevent or repair these malfunctions as they arise is one of the most important measures that we can take to fortify ourselves against disease. In this respect, certain dietary-derived plant compounds are some of our most valuable tools.

Phytochemicals strengthen the body's physiological processes by enhancing the intricate biochemical networks and help to protect them by neutralizing potential toxins. Like the bearings in a machine, these compounds help the whole system to run more smoothly and to resist wear and tear. They increase our chances of maintaining optimal health despite the daily onslaught of both internally produced and ingested toxins and the stresses caused by innate pathogenic processes. These unwelcome agents come in diverse and often unavoidable forms, including environmental pollutants, bacteria, viruses, biochemical malfunctions and genetic idiosyncrasies that make us continuously vulnerable to many different diseases.

In order to strengthen as many strands of this biochemical web as we can, in as many cell and tissue types as possible, we need to flood our bodies with a wide variety of medicinal phytochemicals. For this reason the consumption of an array of spices has such remarkable protective benefits. Individually, most spices contain numerous, potent phytochemicals; collectively, the spices provide a powerful, comprehensive artillery against all of our common, serious chronic diseases.

❯ The Value of Diversity

The protective value that a variety of phytochemicals provides – evidenced so strikingly by the spices – is multifaceted. The first and most obvious reason relates to the range of compounds that are provided by a diet rich in spices and other plants. Clearly, the greater the diversity of medicinal phytochemicals made available to the body, the better equipped it is to use them to curtail pathological processes as they arise. Additionally, because most diseases comprise several pathological mechanisms, the presence of a variety of phytochemicals means that each disease may be curbed in more than one way or at different stages of its development.

The second advantage relating to the intake of a range of plant compounds is in the context of their different bioavailabilities. Powerful antioxidant, anti-inflammatory or other theoretically valuable characteristics do not automatically endow a phytochemical with disease-preventing qualities. Before these substances can be effective, they risk being destroyed in the intestine or, once absorbed into the blood-stream, rendered useless by enzymatic action; some of these are better able to withstand the body's enzymatic and chemical assaults than others. If they manage to avoid degradation, they have still to cross various tissue and cellular barriers – some of which are more selective than others. Relatively few substances, including many antioxidants, are able to cross from the blood into the brain so not all of them are helpful in controlling oxidation and other damaging processes, like inflammation, in the brain. Even when these phytochemicals have successfully accessed the tissues, they must then be able to work in the relevant cellular environment. Some compounds can only function in the "watery" parts of cells, while others are best suited to the lipid-containing areas. A few of them can function in both types of cellular environment.

The third major advantage of diversity lies in the synergic relation-ships between phytochemicals and these manifest themselves in several different ways. One compound may, for example, enhance another's absorption, protect it against degradation by the body or by external toxins, improve its uptake into cells and, finally, enhance its effectiveness at its site of action. In addition, many of the phytochemicals found in different spices have overlapping actions with one another. Therefore the compounds in two different spices may, for instance, both protect against cardiovascular disease or diabetes. They may do this via different mechanisms or may act on the same chemical pathway but in the end they provide a "belt and braces" insurance against the development of chronic diseases. It is far better to have several different compounds working against all of these diseases rather than relying on one or two to provide protection. By consuming an array of phytochemicals we help to ensure the optimal effectiveness of each of these valuable, sometimes overlapping and often complementary substances.

Diversity alone is not, however, sufficient to maximise the overall preventive potential of phytochemicals. For this, we must add consistency to our preventive strategy as pathological processes and toxic substances constantly threaten to undermine our health. If we ensure that our bodies are always well supplied with these valuable, pharmacologically active substances, we dramatically increase the likelihood of thwarting diseases in their earliest stages.

▶ Seasoning Solutions

Diversity and regularity, dual prerequisites for optimising the preventive benefits of phytochemicals, are not as difficult to achieve as one might imagine. Populations that incorporate spices into their traditional dishes have long benefited – in the form of reduced incidences of many different diseases – from an assortment of dietary phytochemicals. Increasing the spice content of the diet does not, of course, guarantee protection against any particular disease. Genetic susceptibility, previous medical history, varying levels of exposure to pathogenic agents and lifestyle habits are all factors that influence health. However, by eating a range of spices and thereby by supplying our bodies with numerous, varied and potent phytochemicals, we can dramatically reduce our chances of developing all of the major chronic diseases.

Unfortunately, incorporating spices into our diets – attractive as it may seem in theory – is by no means straightforward in practice. By our teens, most of us are fairly set in our ways especially when it comes to our food preferences. While enjoying the occasional meal at a Thai or Indian restaurant, most people in the West continue to eat relatively bland meals in their homes. However compelling the evidence attesting to the medicinal value of spices, most of us will be unwilling to start our day with a mouth-burning, eye-watering curry dish that someone in India or Sri Lanka may be in the habit of eating for breakfast. Not only may we be reluctant to incorporate the necessary quantity and variety of spices into our meals, but this may be simply unfeasible if we are too busy to cook and usually resort to pre-prepared meals and take-away food. So, although a few readers may have the resolve and the means to dramatically change their diets, most of us will find the alternative route, in the form of a spice supplement, a much more feasible approach.

▶ Spicy Supplements

Whether added to meals or taken in a tablet or capsule form, the medicinal value of an unadulterated spice is the same. Thus, while it is valuable and indeed pleasurable to incorporate spicier meals into our diets when possible, a spice supplement can ensure we receive all the benefits of a spice-rich diet, irrespective of our dietary preferences. Importantly, because the objective of taking such a pill is to supplement our diets, there are a few key criteria to bear in mind when choosing a formulation.

First, one should not be lured by a product that, for instance, boasts the "strongest" or "most powerful" antioxidant. As discussed earlier, we benefit optimally from the antioxidant and other medicinal properties of plants when we consume a wide variety, rather than a great quantity, of phytochemicals – each substance may work differently, against different pathogenic processes, and in different parts of the body. For preventive purposes, we should also avoid proprietary formulations of spice extracts even though they are useful in treating existing diseases. However, as broad-based prophylactics, spices are better taken in their whole form because of the potential synergism between their myriad compounds. Finally, we should select a supplement that contains a wide range of spices, in quantities based on their content in spice-rich traditional cuisines. Just as we might take a multivitamin and mineral supplement to make up for the micronutrients we would otherwise obtain from an ideally structured diet, so a spice supplement can provide the phytochemicals we would obtain from an optimally spice-rich diet.

▶ Add Spice to Your Life

Adding spices to our diets is one of the most effective measures we can take to assist our bodies in their constant battle against pathogenic assaults and degenerative processes. In doing so, we not only protect ourselves against a variety of debilitating, painful and frequently lethal diseases, but we also enhance our physiological and homeostatic processes and thereby improve our overall feeling of well-being.

This is a measure that we can take immediately, inexpensively and – by using spice supplements – with no inconvenience or disruption to our normal dietary routines. One of the easier ways in which we can take responsibility for our health is by literally "spicing up" our lives.

Glossary of Scientific Terms

adaptogen: A harmless natural product that improves the body's overall physiological functions through a wide range of biochemical actions.

amyloid: A protein that is deposited in tissues under abnormal conditions such as those associated with Alzheimer's disease. Beta-amyloid is a compound derived from amyloid and is the principal component of the plaques found in the brains of Alzheimer's sufferers.

angiogenesis: The formation of new blood vessels.

anorectic: An agent that suppresses the appetite.

antibody: Any of a large number of proteins that act against specific antigens during an immune response.

antigen: A substance foreign to the body that stimulates a cellular or antibody response by the immune system.

antioxidant: A substance that inhibits oxidation; especially those oxidant reactions promoted by free radicals.

apoptosis: The main type of genetically programmed cell death. It is usually a normal, ordered process that generally confers health advantages to multicellular organisms.

atheroma: Abnormal fat deposits in an artery.

atherogenesis: The process that involves the development of atheromatous plaques.

atherosclerosis: A disease process characterized by atheroma and fibrosis of the arterial endothelium. It is one of the causes of arteriosclerosis.

207

arteriosclerosis: A disease process characterized by abnormal thickening and hardening of the arterial walls with associated loss of elasticity that has several known causes.

carcinogen: A cancer-causing agent.

carcinogenic: Capable of causing cancer.

cardiovascular disease: Although technically this term refers to any disease that affects the heart and blood vessels, it is usually used to refer to those diseases related to atherosclerosis (arterial disease) that can cause heart attacks and certain types of strokes.

chelation: The use of a substance to bind with a metal so that it loses its toxic effect and/or is excreted from the body.

cholesterol: A chemical present in cell membranes and body fluids that also functions as a precursor molecule to hormones and other compounds but, when associated with high levels of LDL, may cause atherosclerosis.

COX-2: A type of cyclo-oxygenase enzyme commonly associated with inflammation.

cyclo-oxygenase: An enzyme that catalyzes the conversion of arachidonic acid to prostaglandins and is involved in the "inflammatory cascade" associated with the pain and inflammation connected with arthritis and other diseases.

cytokine: A class of proteins produced, mainly by cells of the immune system, to regulate the functions of the immune system.

endogenous: Something produced by the body itself – see "exogenous".

endothelium: The layer of cells lining the interior surface of all blood vessels. The endothelial layer is involved in the control of blood pressure, blood clotting, atherosclerosis, inflammation and atherogenesis.

epidemiology: The scientific study of factors affecting the health and illness of individuals and populations, and which serves as the foundation for determining relevant preventive and therapeutic interventions.

exogenous: An agent of influence from outside the body – see "endogenous".

fatty acids: Types of naturally occurring and synthetic lipid compounds.

flavonoids: A group of polyphenol, antioxidant compounds that include many plant pigments; the subtypes of which include flavonols, flavones, flavanals, isoflavones and anthocyanadins.

free radical: A reactive endogenous or exogenous molecule containing one or more unpaired electrons that can damage cells, proteins and DNA by altering their chemical structures.

functional food: Any food claimed to have health-promoting and/or disease-preventing properties beyond the function of supplying basic nutrients.

glycemic index (GI): The GI is a ranking system for carbohydrates based on how quickly they are absorbed into the blood stream. Foods with a high GI are absorbed rapidly while those with a low GI are absorbed slowly and, as the latter are associated with lower insulin demands, they are generally considered healthier sources of carbohydrates than those with a high GI.

HDL (High Density Lipoprotein or "good cholesterol"): A lipoprotein that consists of a high proportion of protein with small amounts of triglyceride and cholesterol, high levels of which are associated with a *decreased* risk of developing atherosclerosis.

homeostasis: The characteristic whereby our body regulates and protects its internal environment in order to maintain a stable condition by means of interrelated biochemical mechanisms.

hormesis: A dose response phenomenon whereby a substance that in a high dose inhibits (or is toxic to) a biological process, in a much smaller dose will stimulate (or protect) that same process. Radiation is an agent that demonstrates the property of hormesis.

immunomodulator: A substance that can either enhance or suppress various components of the immune response.

in vitro **research:** Research conducted in a laboratory setting using only biomolecules, cells, tissues or organs.

in vivo **research:** Research conducted on the whole, living organism.

insulin resistance: Reduced sensitivity to insulin by insulin-dependent processes that results in a lowered activity of these processes and/or an increase in insulin production.

ischaemia: A restriction in blood supply usually resulting in damage, dysfunction or death of tissue. Heart attack and ischemic stroke are examples of ischaemic damage to heart muscle and brain tissue respectively.

LDL (Low Density Lipoprotein or "bad cholesterol"): A lipoprotein that consists of a moderate amount of protein with little triglyceride but a high proportion of cholesterol, high levels of which are associated with an increased risk of developing atherosclerosis.

lipid peroxidation: The oxidation of lipids whereby free radicals cause cell damage by "stealing" electrons from the lipids in cell membranes.

lipoproteins: A class of compounds (that include HDL and LDL) composed of proteins and lipids.

macronutrient: An essential nutritional substance such as carbohydrate, fat or protein that is required in relatively large quantities.

metabolic rate: Metabolism per unit time that is calculated by using food and oxygen consumption and the amount of energy produced as heat.

metabolism: The chemical changes and vital processes by which energy is produced and different substances are handled in the body.

metastasis: The spread of a disease (especially cancer) from the primary site to another part of the body.

micronutrient: An element (trace element – e.g. iron) or compound (e.g. a vitamin) that is essential to health in minute quantities.

mitochondria: The organelles in cells responsible for converting organic molecules into energy.

mutagenic: Capable of inducing genetic mutation.

mutation: A change in chromosomal structure that results in biochemical and other changes.

oncogene: A gene that has the potential to cause a healthy cell to become cancerous. Inherited oncogenes predispose some individuals to certain types of cancer.

oxidation: The addition of oxygen or the removal of electrons from a compound.

oxidative stress: A form of stress on the body caused by the cumulative damage done by free radicals unopposed by antioxidants.

oxidizing agent (oxidant): A substance that oxidizes (by accepting electrons) an element or chemical compound.

periodontal: The tissues surrounding a tooth.

phytochemical: Any plant-derived chemical, but generally refers to those that are known to affect biological systems.

polyphenols: A group of antioxidant phytochemicals containing more than one phenol molecule that are responsible for the colouration of some plants.

prostaglandins: Fatty acids that perform a variety of hormone-like functions, such as blood pressure control, but when produced in excess are associated with abnormal inflammatory processes and other pathological conditions.

saturated fats (saturated fatty acids): Fats consisting of triglycerides containing only molecules that have no double bonds between the carbon atoms. Most animal-derived fats (including butter) are saturated as are some plant fats including cocoa butter, coconut oil and palm oil.

synergism (synergy): Interaction of different agents so that the total effect is greater than the sum of the individual effects.

telomere: A region of highly repetitive DNA at the end of a chromosome that functions as a disposable buffer to prevent the loss of important genetic information. The loss of telomeres is thought to be linked to aging.

thermogenesis: The process of heat production caused primarily by the metabolism of fatty acids and is related to the metabolic rate. The higher the metabolic rate the more free fatty acids are broken down to produce heat.

triglyceride: A group of lipids that are widespread in adipose tissues and circulate in the blood in the form of lipoproteins. High triglyceride levels are associated with increased risk of developing atherosclerosis.

tumourigenic: Capable of producing tumours (cf. *carcinogenic*).

unsaturated fats (unsaturated fatty acids): Fats having one or more double bonds between the carbon atoms. Most plant and fish oils contain unsaturated fatty acids. They are *monounsaturated* if each contains one double bond (e.g. olive oil) or *polyunsaturated* if they contain more than one double bond (e.g. canola oil, sunflower oil).

Index

213

R

red meat 66, 108, 169, 170
red peppers 114, **175–176**
red wine 19, *78*, *81*, 157
refined foods 42
respiratory infections 190
resveratrol 19, 108, 157, 158
rheumatoid arthritis 61, *118*
Roaccutane 40
rosemary **159–160**
  anticancer properties 58, 66, *78*, *81*, 159
  anti-inflammatory properties 88, 91,
    119, 160
  antimicrobial properties 62
  benefits for Alzheimer's disease 48, 102,
    103, 160
  blood thinning properties 59
  cardioprotective action 37, 162
  inhibits atherogenesis *90*, 160
  lowers blood lipid levels 88, *90*, 160
  reduces platelet aggregation *90*, 91, 160
  reduces platelet stickiness 88
  source of antioxidants 91, 160
rosmarinic acid 160, 162, 164, 193, 194
rutin 188

S

sage 19, 55, 74, 119
salicylates **120–123**, 130, 159, 163, 188
salicylic acid 120, 122, 123, 195
scientific evidence 14–16
selenium 152
shingles 176
shogaol 140
Siamese ginger 65–66
smoking 18, 26, 70, 85, 86, 107, *118*, 167
soy **171–174**
  anticancer properties 58, *78*, *82*, *83*,
    171–172
  benefits for Alzheimer's disease 173
  benefits for menopause 174
  benefits for osteoporosis 173
  genistein 48, 65, 172, 173, 174
  inhibits atherogenesis *90*, 172
  lowers blood lipid levels 88, *90*, 91, 172
  plant food not spice 14

source of salicylates 121
spice (definition) 14
spices
  effect of climate 34–35
  flavours 30–32
  health benefits 20–30, 200–201
  importance of diversity 201–203
  key medicinal properties *56*
  mechanisms 53–68
  preservatives 33–34
  safety and risk factors 44–50
  synergism 47–48, *56*, 64–66, 202–203
star anise 88, 91, **195**
statins 54, 85, 88, 92
sticky platelets 54, 59, 85, 86, 88, 89,
  90, 145
stomach cancer 139, 142, 144, 169, 184
stomach ulcers 28, 139, 142, 144, 182
strokes 91, 122
sulphorane 72, 170
sunlight 70, 77, 107
superoxide dismutase 136, 141, 156, 180
supplements 17, 204–205
survivin 158
synergism 47–48, *56*, 64–66, 202–203
synthetic seasonings 36

T

tamoxifen 54, 65, 128, 129
tangeretin 166
tarragon 34, 121, **195**
thyme **163–164**
  anticancer properties 163
  anti-inflammatory properties 88, 91,
    119, 164
  antimicrobial properties 34, 62
  blood thinning properties 59
  inhibits atherosclerosis 164
  lowers blood lipid levels 88, *90*, 91, 164
  reduces platelet aggregation *90*, 91
  reduces platelet stickiness 88, 164
  source of antioxidants 55, 74, 119
thymol 164
toxin neutralisation *56*, 66–67, 156
triglyceride levels 58, 86, 87–88, 134, 136
turmeric **127–131**

References

Book and journal references for *Medicinal Seasonings* may be found on the website: www.medicinalseasonings.com

About the Author

For the past thirty years Keith Scott has worked as a medical doctor in both city and rural practices in Southern Africa, the United Kingdom and New Zealand.

During that period he has incorporated complementary medicine into his medical practice and has co-authored two other books including the best selling, *Natural Home Pharmacy*. Both books have been translated into several languages. Dr. Scott has appeared on numerous TV and radio programs and has written health related articles for newspapers and magazines.

He has conducted courses for doctors interested in complementary medicine and was a member of a task force advising the New Zealand government on complementary therapies.

Dr. Scott was the founding president of the New Zealand Biological Producers' Council, an NGO that certifies organically grown produce in New Zealand.

For several years he ran a medical practice in Botswana that involved flying to remote villages where, before antiretroviral drugs became available, he successfully used complementary medical modalities to help treat the large number of his patients who were stricken with HIV/AIDS.

Dr Scott lives and works in Cape Town, South Africa.

www.medicinalseasonings.com